PHŒNIX RISING

PH**O**ENIX
RISING

Stories of Remarkable Women
Walking Through Fire

KRISTEN MOELLER &
LESLIE APLIN WHARTON

New York

PHOENIX RISING

Stories of Remarkable Women Walking Through Fire

© 2016 KRISTEN MOELLER & LESLIE APLIN WHARTON.

Published in New York, New York, by Morgan James Publishing. Morgan James and The Entrepreneurial Publisher are trademarks of Morgan James, LLC. www.MorganJamesPublishing.com

The Morgan James Speakers Group can bring authors to your live event. For more information or to book an event visit The Morgan James Speakers Group at www.TheMorganJamesSpeakersGroup.com.

A **free** eBook edition is available with the purchase of this print book.

CLEARLY PRINT YOUR NAME ABOVE IN UPPER CASE
Instructions to claim your free eBook edition:
1. Download the BitLit app for Android or iOS
2. Write your name in **UPPER CASE** on the line
3. Use the BitLit app to submit a photo
4. Download your eBook to any device

ISBN 978-1-63047-723-3 paperback
ISBN 978-1-63047-724-0 eBook
Library of Congress Control Number:
2015912340

Cover Photo by:
Jessica Wilson

Cover Design by:
Rachel Lopez
www.r2cdesign.com

Interior Design by:
Bonnie Bushman
The Whole Caboodle Graphic Design

In an effort to support local communities and raise awareness and funds, Morgan James Publishing donates a percentage of all book sales for the life of each book to Habitat for Humanity Peninsula and Greater Williamsburg.

Get involved today, visit
www.MorganJamesBuilds.com

To our fellow firewalkers…
may we all keep on walking

CONTENTS

Foreword   *ix*

Introduction   *xiii*

Phoenix Rising   *Leslie Aplin Wharton*   1

I Know the Color Gray   *Jenn Nolte*   7

Here Be Dragons   *Barbara Nickless*   9

After Disaster, Beauty Remains   *Kendra Eucker*   17

Life on Melvina Hill   *Ann Lansing*   21

No Ordinary Fire   *Sandi Yukman*   27

My Paradise   *Louise Creager*   33

Shades   *Beth Cutter*   39

The 503: The Things We Leave Behind   *Melissa Fry*   41

Starting Over   *Jackie Klausmeyer*   51

Rising from the Ashes   *Yvette Trantham*   59

The Dream   *Jenn Nolte*   65

Canyon Spirit   *Bonnie Antich*   75

Irreplaceable Things   *Susan Ruane McConnell*   81

Tempered, Forged, Tensiled FREE   *Astrid*   89

Fire on the Mountain   *Cheryl Delany*   91
The Wildfire of Birth   *Amanda DeAngelis*   97
The Thoughtful Side of Insanity   *AnnMarie Arbo*   103
For Better or for Worse   *Linda Masterson*   107
Finding Meaning in the Fire   *Bethany Trantham*   115
Walking through Fire   *Kristen Moeller*   121

About the Contributors   129
About the Authors   135
Photo Album   137
Phoenix Rising Fund   155

FOREWORD

What would you take if you had five minutes to flee from your home? What would you say if you knew your life was ending? And if it didn't, if disaster spared your life but ruined most of its trappings, what then? These are the questions lived and explored in these pages.

Many of us, if we're lucky, have only paused to consider such hypotheticals while watching news of wildfires or floods or tornadoes—terrified people seeking refuge, heartbroken homeowners surveying their losses, bereaved families grieving their loved ones. But we only see fragmented snapshots of those moments.

In this gem of a book written by women united by wildfire, we have the privilege of stepping into those moments to stand in the hallways of their shock and fear, grief and disorientation, and then, armed with the wisdom of retrospection, walking out into whatever comes next. It's nothing less than being witness to the very act of creation itself: from chaos, order; from nothingness, something. Kind of like fire and the regeneration that follows.

I've heard that during an explosion, there's a moment when all of the pieces that have been blown apart seem to freeze and hang suspended in the air. It's similar when the entire container of your life ceases to exist—the reeling sense of dislocation, as if you're just floating, alone and disjointed. In addition to wildfire itself, that experience and what comes after it is what the stories you're about to read have in common.

The authors, either born in or drawn to the West's vast spaces and galloping wilderness, demonstrate the unique blend of grit and vulnerability, doggedness and reflection, so characteristic of the region's most memorable women (think shooter Annie Oakley, frontier novelist Willa Cather, and Cherokee Chief Wilma Mankiller). All of them respond differently to their fire experience, but their responses have common themes: First, they adhere to the old saying that one of them quotes, "When the going gets tough, the tough get going." This means sprinting from flames leading a beloved horse, working tirelessly as a firefighter to save homes, searching for an interim home capable of accommodating not only a family but also a troupe of dogs, horses and ducks, or digging for remnants of a cherished home before clearing away the rubble to rebuild.

Second, these women search for meaning amid so many questions: What is home when it's lost? Who are we without the items we have collected and carried with us through the years—a comfortable old Saints t-shirt from New Orleans, a glamorous Diane Von Furstenberg coat, or an ice cream maker and knitted chair covers inherited from a grandmother? Sifting through ash is also sifting through memory. Whatever we choose to bring with us and the meaning we make of it, be it a shard of green pottery, a charred totem pole, or the recollection of belonging somewhere, will help to determine who we become.

Third, these women show us resilience. Most of us know the metaphor of the lodgepole pine, which requires wildfire for the cones to open and release seeds. That's an apt starting point for the resilience shown in these stories, but it's only the beginning. Because the authors don't merely keep going, perpetuating life in rote numbness. No. They succeed in maintaining their hearts, their vibrance, their joy. We can take inspiration in the way they live this truth: No matter how unfair this world may be, it's up to us to figure out how to be happy and productive while living in it. No one can fix it for us, and no one can do that for us. That central fact of life will never change for any of us as long as we're here, no matter the particular circumstance, whether wildfire or anything else (By the time anyone turns 40 or 50, they've gone through at least one explosion that has destroyed the container of their life: Betrayal. Divorce. Illness. Shattered dreams of varied stripes and colors). It's the constant challenge, and the constant opportunity. To keep going *and* keep finding joy, no matter how unjust the world or how undesirable our lives may seem at any moment.

Kurt Vonnegut wrote, "*Be soft. Do not let the world make you hard. Do not let the pain make you hate. Do not let the bitterness steal your sweetness. Take pride that even though the rest of the world may disagree, you still believe it to be a beautiful place.*"

These women are a shining example of that, whether after the fires they moved to a cool, moist place, starred in a television show, found a new home in the city or rebuilt a home where their old one once stood.

My favorite part of reading their stories is that I felt as if I were gathered round a fire with a favorite group of women. When it comes to withstanding and making meaning of the most painful twists of this mysterious life, or enjoying its surprising rewards, nothing compares to the company of other women and their stories. Fire and life are alike in their ability to warm and sustain, as well as damage and ruin, and we can't have one power without the other. It's the same with our personalities—

the frailties and flaws co-exist with the attributes and strengths. They're inextricable. Which is why the Buddhists recommend sitting with the undesirable—making friends with it, in a sense—without trying to erase or resist it. While it's tempting to write about "rising from the ash" as some redemptive tale in which everything becomes good again, that's not what life is. It's about holding the good and the bad, the beautiful and the terrible, and fashioning a meaningful existence filled with love along the way. Doing that in the company of other women makes the pain more bearable and the beauty more divine. And that's the greatest gift of this book.

—**Megan Feldman Bettencourt**

Megan Feldman Bettencourt is a Denver-based, award-winning journalist whose work has appeared in publications including The San Francisco Chronicle, Newsday, Glamour, Details, and Southwest: The Magazine. She is the author of Triumph of the Heart: Forgiveness in an Unforgiving World (Penguin 2015), which explores forgiveness through memoir, stories and science. You can visit her at www.meganfeldman.com.

INTRODUCTION

Those of us who have experienced grief, or lived through intense trauma, know that healing has no definitive path. Walking through grief is not a straight line, no matter how much we wish it were. Instead, it's often rocky terrain with many unexpected bumps in the road. The other side of grief is not a place of arrival but merely a momentary resting place. Yet healing is possible, and one day we smile again.

The healing balm in these stories comes from many sources—time spent in nature, the comfort of counselors, a belief in God—or another form of a higher power—love from family or friends, pets, yoga, writing, the wisdom of turning inward, as well as bouts of screaming and crying. We have discovered that true healing ultimately arises from our deepest core, even though trauma can make us question even that.

Before we met, we both craved a connection with other women who had walked through fire. We longed for a storytelling society where women gathered together in a circle to share, support, and give strength.

We sought out women who had been writing their own tales after their experiences with fire. Intuitively, we knew these writings held a rare and remarkable gift. We recognized the power of sharing our journeys of how fire forged our souls, left us blackened and scarred, yet more beautiful than ever.

The vision for this book arose like a flame for each of us, and then it slowly burned out when we realized that for many women, in the early days after their fires, it was too soon to share. Hearts were too tender and raw; memories too painful. We remembered those days, consumed with finding a place to live and clothes to wear, when we didn't have space for much else. Somewhat dismayed, we practically abandoned the idea of collecting stories. (Leslie was hard at work focusing her attention on her memoir about the fire, *Edge of Next*, while Kristen was finishing and publishing her second book, *What Are You Waiting For? Learn How to Rise to the Occasion of Your Life.*)

Then one fateful day, we met through a phone call and immediately recognized a sisterhood. We shared and cried and then confessed that we both imagined the concept for this book. For each of us, writing became a grounding force after losing our homes. It kept us sane. It kept us connected to something larger than ourselves. And it kept us moving forward.

Working as partners has been a gift. Neither of us could have completed this project alone while we sought to pull our own lives together, find new places to call home, finish the reams of insurance paperwork, and finally heal.

The wisdom in this book comes from women of varying ages, backgrounds, and experiences. They share a medley of therapeutic paths, diverse spiritual beliefs, and the common thread of healing through the passage of time. Some women lost their homes, some stood by helplessly as they watched their neighbors lose theirs, some fought fires, and others helped mend broken hearts. We received stories from award-winning authors and from those who had never written before. No matter our differences, we found we had much in common, and though our healing paths varied, our hearts overlapped.

We call the women in these stories "firewalkers." Firewalkers are people who have walked through the fires of life, whether literal or metaphorical, and emerge with a deeper understanding of themselves and the world. Our collection of firewalkers who share their stories were literally transformed by fire. Yet many people live through a traumatic event that alters them forever, such as illness, accidents, divorce, natural disasters, death of a loved one, abuse, or war. No matter your background or the version of fire you have walked through in life, we hope these stories will bring you comfort in knowing you are not alone in your journey.

A suggestion: if you buy this book for a firewalker, giftwrap it in beautiful paper. Tell them what's inside, but let them open it only when they're ready. It's questionable whether or not they will open it the first year after their fire—and if they do, they may not be able to finish reading it. The second year after the fire they'll love it. They'll read each story and cry and cry. Then they will read it again.

As they read, they will be reassured that they are not crazy, and their tears will cleanse their pain. The third year they may or may not want to read the book or think about fire. Instead, they'll need to bask in joy. For most of the women in the book, we still don't know what the fourth year of healing will bring. The experience of fire continues to transform us. Some of us still aren't sure who we will be on the other side.

The women in these pages will always be our heroes and part of our clan. We thank them for sharing their writing and opening our hearts. We have all lived through a horrendous experience that dapples the background of our lives and colors it with both strength and sadness. We hope these stories will help others understand what it takes to be a firewalker.

So, in the end, the phoenix rises, but we have found through experience that it takes its own sweet time.

PHOENIX RISING

LESLIE APLIN WHARTON

R ight after the fire, I detested the image of the phoenix rising, and it was all around me. My friend gave me a jade necklace with a carved phoenix. The old milk truck sitting in a field at the base of our canyon was painted with a phoenix rising up from flames. It was plastered with encouraging words like—we will rebuild— we are strong. We were not strong. We were not beautifully transformed creatures rising out of the ashes. We were more like marshmallows burnt by flames—black and crispy on the outside, sweet and gooey on the inside, too hot to touch. If you didn't hold us gently and wait for us to cool down, we might burn you and you'd have to spit us out.

My husband and I built our house, with our own hands, and then it was gone. Having no children, our house was my baby. I gave birth to it and nurtured it for eighteen years. The image of the phoenix pressured me to be strong and to rise out of the ashes, but I wasn't strong. I was a

1

mess while gathering debris at my house site to take to the dump. My hand-me-down clothes were black with soot; I had char on my face, and my eyes were red and swollen. I was grieving. I wanted to lie down forever to be covered by ash.

The High Park fire destroyed 259 houses and over three hundred other structures; 87,000 acres of plants and trees—and one woman—lost their lives. They don't report the number of animals lost, whether pets or wild, some of which returned, and some never did. We lost our lives as we knew them, and we fled. People said we were brave to leave Colorado and start a new life in Washington State. It might have been braver for us to stay and rebuild on our land. We just couldn't do it.

We had built that house, lived that life, and climbed those mountains. We were scared of fire and climate change, and we suffered from the trauma it left in our lives. Intense heat and smoke tormented us for weeks as we waited for the fire to be over. After we cleaned up our house site and said good-bye to friends, we moved to western Washington where it is cool and moist.

For a year after the fire, we went into survival mode. Like deer in the headlights of a car, we were scared and confused. Our brains literally didn't work right. We were reduced to searching for the basics—food, shelter, clothes, tools, and jobs. It took a physical toil on us. Stress hormones surged through our bodies. We either ate too much or couldn't eat; we couldn't sleep or we slept too much—and we had nightmares. My husband had hives all over his body for months and months. I drank too much, hoping to erase myself. I had what I call spontaneous weeping.

A vision of the house, a hug from a friend, a brokenhearted love song, or anything could make me weep at any moment. At times we lashed out at each other and the people we loved most. Nothing could be taken lightly. We were left broken by a dream fulfilled, then shattered.

One of the most difficult times for us was seven months after the fire when everyone thought we should be better. We had all the physical belongings we needed to live, but we realized it was not enough. We had to find peace again, which is more difficult than finding furniture. I am at peace again now three years later.

Insurance didn't replace what we lost or sooth us emotionally, but insurance money enabled us to move and buy a home. Grateful for our insurance and the kindness that friends and strangers showed us, we now send small checks to people who lose their home in a disaster only to find out later that their insurance does not cover them. We struggle with rebuilding careers in our fifties and worry about money, but we do not worry about love. Money from insurance can buy a house, but it is the love from family and friends that makes it a home.

On the two-year anniversary of the fire, we returned to Colorado to visit friends, work on our land, and gather with some of the women in this book to read poems and stories to the public. When we first returned to our house site, we stood still on the land and looked out at the black trees surrounding us. We felt sad for a life we no longer had, but at that instant an eagle flew by, soaring right above us. It looked at us as if to say, "What are you doing on my land?" It circled three times. Like our friends, it reassured us that everything is okay, because we have a new life now—and it promised to watch over the land.

I no longer feel like a marshmallow, thank goodness, and the image of the phoenix is now comforting. But I still can't picture myself as a phoenix rising. Instead, I resonate with the bald eagle. Eagles are thought to be courageous. But their strength has little to do with courage; they simply do what they need to do to survive. Eagles rest in the large evergreen trees by my new house and feed off salmon spawning in the nearby river.

This spring, when I was planting trees in the rain, I caught sight of two huge eagles in the sky. One of them had a wingspan of at least six feet. I dropped my shovel and lay down on my back. I spread my arms wide open in the wet meadow grass. My hair was damp with fresh rainwater, and with my head on the cool earth, I lay still. I watched as the eagles majestically rode currents of air. They soared high as they searched for small creatures in the meadow grass. The eagles flew back and forth across the gray blue sky between clouds like sailboats tacking between islands in the bay. They hunted and I didn't dare move. I watched in awe until they disappeared from sight behind the tall crooked trees on the horizon.

In Native American culture, bald eagles are messengers between the spirit world and the human world. Since the fire, I spend more time in the spirit world. I listen to the trees, I wade in the rivers, and I watch the rising tides on the coast. The message the spirits send to the human race is *take care of the earth, keep it clean; your life depends on it.* The message we send to the spirits is *forgive us.*

Mark and I don't fly, but while sitting in bed drinking coffee, our minds soar and we catch the slightest currents of energy. We picture our whole lives laid out exposed before us. At times it can be overwhelming. We pinpoint with survivor instincts, in sharp focus, the tiniest chance for food, and we sweep down to grab it with our sharp talons. We bought a freezer and we fill it with salmon from the rivers and berries from our meadow, and I freeze veggies from a local farm I work for. We gather firewood to keep warm in the winter.

The other day I was walking in the yard after planting hollyhocks and heard a loud sound above me. Startled, I looked up to see the two huge bald eagles that live on our land riding on top of each other as they fell from the sky. They made a raucous commotion; it was a huge, dark mass of flailing wings, and at first I thought the eagles were fighting. Instinctively, I ducked and then yelled for Mark, who was in the garage. Then I reasoned that the pair was mating and I quieted. I watched as they descended from the sky, right above my head, latched together at the claws. They tried to fly but couldn't. Their wings flapped together, thrashing loudly, the bottom wings hitting the top wings and the top wings hitting the bottom wings.

They crashed into our large birch tree while trying to perch on a branch, but they were unbalanced and focused only on love, so they tumbled out of the tree and landed on the ground ten feet in front of me. They quickly finished mating and flew away. I ran to tell Mark. I knew they had been sent to me as a message for this story, and I pondered, searching for that message.

It says to me—give up control for love. Cling to what I love, hold on tight, even if it causes me to fall, plummet, leaving me vulnerable. It may be that in the most helpless, exposed position, I will find love deepening. Forget about the Buddhist lesson of detachment and instead attach, furiously. Serenity is not what I need to find; I need passion.

Eagles mate for life. They build enormous nests and add to them each year. Their nests can weigh over a ton. Occasionally, the tree with their heavy nest falls down and they have to build another nest. Mark and I like our new nest in our new house and will improve it as long as we live here. I hope that as we add bits of our creativity to this place, we will grow to love it and that we will allow ourselves to risk intense attachment to home once again.

Our love for each other has deepened as we recover from the fire. Losing our home and belongings taught us that love is the most important possession. Love is really all that matters. If trauma destroys love by death or by stress that is a true tragedy. Anyone living through a disaster should surround themselves with love and hold on tight.

Don't let stress ruin your relationships. Give yourself time; fear and anger will dissipate and love will multiply. Let love envelope you in its tight grip and rest there, when you're not too busy searching for food and shelter.

I KNOW THE COLOR GRAY

JENN NOLTE

I know the color gray, for the ash falling out of the orange haze of sky
For the smoke thirteen miles away on that June day
For the lights flashing on the dirt road, for a last pause and then a
    flurry of away
I know the color red, for the next morning the flames consuming all in
    its way
For the fire line coming closer, no longer thirteen miles away
For the constant whir in the sky, of hopes of water having the final say
For the winds to shift, to stop their merciless howl
I know the color black, for the charred bark of trees loved so much,
    their shelter lost
For the long earned love of timbers only now to barely register as dust

For the smoke tinged air, of the dark landscape forever changed
What to do now—the question amidst all the tears
I know the color brown, as the earth is scraped away, along with it a
    piece of my soul
For nothing left except the haunting smell in the air
For the anticipated love of place dissolved into despair
I know the color green as grasses that color the ridge that next year
For the resolve to try again, to dream again
I know the color yellow as petals that wave in the gentle wind, rising
    toward the sky
For the miracles of a tiny new cactus in between blackened rocks
For the bird calls echoing through the bare branches of a dead tree
For the new smells of freshly cut wooden beams
I know the color of hope as it rises to form a new beginning the
    year after
Overcoming the flame, the downpours, the setbacks, the frustrations
For the joy at the wild turkeys return, for the beautiful fox never
    before seen
For the worn hands laboring with natural stone
For the coming home, for the house that now stands proud
On our ridge of possibilities bought so long ago

HERE BE DRAGONS

BARBARA NICKLESS

On my desk, before it burned, I had a map. A papyrus-yellow sketch of a Lenox globe from the 1500s. I'd chosen this map because it was made during the Age of Exploration when Europeans ventured to the four corners of the globe—into the dark heart of Africa, the wilds of the Atlantic, out among the islands of the Pacific, and across the vast New World.

Perhaps, unconsciously I think, I also chose the map for its warning to sailors— *hic sunt dracones*. Here be dragons. Travel past the edges of the known world, the cartographers warned, and you might not come back.

I'd placed the map on my desk in the hope it would inspire me to risk my own uncharted territories—be they places with real geography or the terra incognita of my heart. But it had been years since I'd known how to face down the dragons. For twelve months, until I rolled it up and tucked it away, the map lay in quiet rebuke, reminding me of everything I feared to do.

Also on my desk, before it burned, was a photo of my mother. Whenever I studied her guarded expression, distressingly cautious for a child of only three or four, the photo assured me that the world my mother lived in had always held dragons. Sometimes, in a half-dreaming state, I would merge the map and my mother's photograph until she was the one offering caution.

"Be careful, honey," I'd imagine her saying. "There are dragons."

Then an embellishment I knew she would have offered if she'd known about my Lenox map.

"Be careful, honey. There are dragons."

Pause.

"Fire-breathing dragons."

My mother prized being safe over living large. *Better safe than sorry* was her motto. She had a convert's fervor when it came to safeguarding her family against life's calamities. She believed in snakebite kits and overcooked pork. She swore by sanitizing soaps and insect repellent. As a general rule, we steered clear of swimming pools and contact sports.

She told me to always pack snow boots and a jacket in the trunk of the car because you just never know. She debated whether—in the event of a fire—I should have a ladder near my window. Only her worry that I would escape the flames to fall to my death ended that.

Like most kids raised in a safe and healthy home, I ran heedless into the world. Head back, mouth wide open, the wind in my hair. I roamed far and wide, collecting pebbles and sticks and scrapes and bumps. I brought home lizards and fell down holes and rode my bike in places that would have made my mother drop dead in horror had she known.

Through it all I emerged mainly unscathed, rarely needing more than a tetanus shot or an ice pack. This should have been enough to convince my mother that she was now safe. That the dragons had left the enchanted forest and retreated to their caves.

But what she knew and I didn't yet know is that the dragons are patient.

My mother grew up poor in Athens, Tennessee, during the Great Depression. Her father was moody and violent, an alcoholic with thwarted dreams of success.

When my mother was nine, he ordered her and her siblings to line up in the backyard, each with an apple atop their head. He had a bow and a few arrows. While her brothers and sisters tearfully took their places, my mother ducked around the corner of the house and fled into the fields.

Fortunately for my cousins-yet-to-be, my grandmother talked her husband down and took his arrows.

Later, my grandfather called my mother a coward for running away. But my mother was the brave one. It is hard to defy a dragon.

I think my mother fell in love with my father in part because he was safe. He didn't drink. He didn't swear. He never hit her. The pair settled into a 1950s idyll of marriage and children and a series of faithful dogs. Money was tight, but they were happy.

But every night, she checked the stove, checked the oven, and locked the doors and windows tight.

As I grew, my mother wanted to keep me close. But I longed for a life of adventure. College in a faraway place, then a stint in the Peace Corps followed by work in the diplomatic arena. Ultimately, I planned to settle somewhere interesting, an ex-patriot in an exotic land, my own Age of Exploration nicely resolved in permanent exile.

But when my mother discouraged my college choices—too far, bad neighborhood, too expensive, too intimidating—I surprised myself and capitulated. Somewhere along the line, in the stretch of years from ten to seventeen, the dragons had crept in on cats' feet, slipping unnoticed past my mother and altering me forever. My mother's understanding of monsters was now my own, the fear like a plague in my blood.

I stayed close to home during college, took a safe, reasonable job, and settled quietly into my own life of marriage and home and children.

And every night, like my mother, I checked the stove, checked the oven, and locked the doors and windows tight.

For sailors in the Age of Discovery, exploring the world in their frail, proud ships must have been their version of a particularly addictive form of crack cocaine. Which is to say, adventuring was a lethally appealing activity. While storms, cannibals, and man-eating tigers made a dent in the population of European sailors, their own ignorance killed many of them; an estimated two million sailors died of scurvy between 1500 and 1800.

I like to imagine the mapmakers sitting safely in their workshops, pouring over notes and sketches of the known world and wanting, in some small way, to help those brave or hapless men by drawing warnings on their maps: sea serpents and basilisks and the words *hic sunt dracones*.

After my mother's fears seeped into me, I would have made a great medieval cartographer. Earnest and dedicated. Cautious and precise. Reveling in the small, safe pleasures of a confined space while dreaming of bigger things.

But though I stayed vigilant during those years, watching over my family, I could not keep us safe. For here is a truth: If you don't risk the dragons, the dragons will come to you.

Try to keep them from the gate, and they will dig under the walls.

In the summer of 2012, our house burned to the ground in a wildfire. We escaped with little more than the clothes on our backs. My quiet, settled life became one of public mourning, and the ensuing weeks and months were taken up with trying to keep things normal for my family while recreating some semblance of home.

The dragons, once done burning down our home, didn't return immediately. They bided their time until the first frantic months were behind us, waited until we had a place to live and enough bedding, dishes and towels to suffice, and we had space to breathe and think.

Then began the time I think of as the Stumbling.

Rats, in repeated experiments, have shown that when subjected to random electric shocks, they suffer greater depression and trauma than rats that experience consistently applied shocks. It's the terror generated by not knowing when the next dragon is coming that keeps our minds and bodies in perpetual stress.

My family had suffered other sorrows, other struggles. The fire was only the most public. And so, like those rats, I'd learned that random, unexpected disasters have a cumulative effect. The more monsters life tosses at you, the more fearful you become of the next onslaught. Your adrenaline surges over minor alarms, digestion shuts down, your blood pressure spikes with every late-night ring of the phone, and life becomes one of waiting for the next shoe to drop.

During the Stumbling, so named for both my constant bumping into unfamiliar furniture and how my mind couldn't find a clear path, insomnia became my companion. An unwelcome guest that I nonetheless had to allow in. I took to roaming our rental house at night, faltering in the dark through unaccustomed rooms. Ever vigilant, I checked doors and windows, made sure my mother's wedding ring was still next to the sink, that the cat hadn't been inadvertently locked outside, and that my children were abed.

But for all my vigilance, I was drowning. My careful—one could say neurotic—attention had not served any better than my mother's. The dragons had taken our home, my children's security, a lifetime of treasures. We had sailed right off the edge of the world and had no map to lead us back.

The one journey my mother wished to make before she died was to see the orchids in Hawaii. But with age, her fears grew up around her like the vines devouring Sleeping Beauty's castle. She never went.

After the wildfire, I thought a lot about this. Had my mother dreamed broken dreams of soft-petaled orchids as she lay dying in hospice?

And was this what she wanted for me?

Then one day, while I was searching my father's house, I found another childhood photo of my mother.

In this one, she is impish, unposed, one hand reached awkwardly toward her younger sister as if to pull a blond curl. She still carries a wounding in her eyes; indeed, of all the children in the photograph, only the baby looks happy.

But she isn't drowning. There is a feistiness in her I didn't know she possessed. I look at that hand sneaking toward her sister's head of curls and know that although she lived with a monster, she could still work a little playful deviltry of her own. Before her dragons engulfed her, my mother was just a little girl who dreamed, like all little girls, of grand adventures.

As I studied this second photograph, I realized I'd learned something my mother had lost along the way: Sometimes the cartographer must venture forth and confront the dragons in order to fill in the terra incognita of his maps. That he must go even when, like those long-ago sailors, he *knows* there are dragons.

In truth, there is no other way to fully live our lives or to understand ourselves. It is how we grow. Weight applied to muscle strengthens the bones. A bone, once broken, heals back stronger. And pain, like bones, can grow us from the inside out.

On my new desk in our new home, are maps. Books about exploration fill my shelves. Travel magazines are piled on the floor. No longer a quiet rebuke, these things are a reminder that the dragons must be faced.

I hope—I believe—I am learning to be brave again. To run not-quite-heedless into the world, head back, mouth open, the wind in my hair.

As I venture out into my own Age of Discovery, I will carry my mother's cautions with me. If I end up floating down the Nile, you can bet that my cell phone will be charged, I'll carry a snakebite kit, and I'll have a jacket—because you just never know.

But I'm going. It is time. It is past time.

Now, I don't think if my mother were alive she'd approve. She'd worry about heat stroke and terrorists and crocodiles.

There are dragons, she'd say.

And she'd be right.

But here is what I think would happen once she saw my determination. She'd realize that a life cannot be well lived until we don our armor and sharpen our swords and march out under a pitiless sky to face the dragons. To vanquish them or—if need be—to die trying. With that realization, she'd hug me through her tears, and as I walked out the door, she'd whisper in my ear.

Safe journey, my love.

Godspeed.

And don't forget your sunscreen.

AFTER DISASTER, BEAUTY REMAINS

KENDRA EUCKER

A s another anniversary of the Lower North Fork fire approaches, again I struggle to understand why bad things have to happen. That day was one of the worst of my life. Never before have I worried so much about my family. Never have I thought about my life ending.

Seeing my life flash before my eyes was unsettling. In that moment, I didn't think only of things I had done wrong, I thought about all the things I had never done at all. I thought about all the goals I had yet to accomplish. I thought about the people that matter most in my life. I thought about all the words I had left unsaid.

This was one of the few times in my life that I prayed. As the flames engulfed the land and sky around me, I prayed that God, or some higher power, would keep my family safe. I prayed that my siblings and friends would accomplish their goals and find love. I prayed that the man I loved would find his way, fall in love with someone amazing, and live a long happy life.

I opened my eyes and realized how much I had taken for granted. Not hearing my screams, the firefighters kept driving and I almost accepted my fate. Almost. In a split second, I chose to fight. I couldn't bear not having the chance to make an impact on the world. I couldn't stand the thought of leaving behind all the people who I loved so dearly.

I ran. Without breathing, I ran as fast as I could. I blocked out the explosions, the thick black smoke, the hot air, and the embers burning my skin. I had to reach the firefighters. I had to save my family. I had to save my dad, my mom, my little brother, our horses, our dogs, and our cat.

In that instant, I had to make decisions that would affect my life forever. I ran alongside my dad's truck with one of my horses. My dad drove through the fence, and my mom followed in her Jeep. Both vehicles were filled with our animals. The only horse I was able to grab, Cimarron, was running right behind me. The air became so thick we could no longer run. The air was so black that we could not see. Embers were landing on my arms and burning Cimmi's fur.

We were stuck and couldn't move any further. I looked into his eyes and saw a fear I had never seen before. I saw the orange flames in his eyes as my dad begged me to let him go and get in the truck. I kissed his nose one more time before I threw his lead and screamed, "RUN, CIMMI, RUN."

My dad drove violently. The black smoke made it impossible to see as we flew over boulders and around trees. The flames were getting closer and the air was getting hotter as we crashed into the ditch. I saw the flames closing in around us. I looked down and saw the fire trucks... they were leaving! Jumping out of the truck, I ran and screamed like I never had before. When the fireman finally heard my screams, I broke down. I had never been so grateful in my life.

I haven't forgotten a single thought or memory from that day.

I still think about my neighbors who lost their lives. I still think about my neighbors who lost their homes and those that lost their pets.

Driving home is a constant reminder of what happened. When I think back to that day, I try to forget running through the flames thinking my family was going to die. I try to block out those horrifying memories of watching the flames engulf the entire mountain. I try to look back and think about how lucky we were, my family and I. We had someone watching over us that day.

Going through all these memories isn't easy for me, but I know that I have gained a better understanding of life. We forget how precious life is. We take for granted the things we value most. Life is so unpredictable and we never know how much time we have left.

Please tell your friends and family that you love them. Go out and do everything you can in this world, see everything. At the end of the day, have no regrets. Life is short and you never know when yours is ending.

None of us will ever forget March 26, 2012. We will move forward and learn from this tragedy. Life is not over. From the ashes we pick ourselves up, life returns, and once again our world is restored with beauty.

LIFE ON MELVINA HILL

ANN LANSING

I lived in a house my husband and I built in Four Mile Canyon outside of Boulder, Colorado, from the time I was twenty-five until it burned in the Four Mile fire of September 2010, right before my sixty-second birthday. The hill we lived on was named Melvina Hill because of the Melvina Gold Mine, which was named after the wife of the original gold miner. My daughter, Melvina, was born in our house and named after the hill we loved so much. She was thirty-three at the time of the fire. My nineteen-year-old son, Joey, lived his whole life there. My second husband had been there with me for twenty-eight years. All those years, I lived with the knowledge that we could lose everything to fire. It was only in the last few years that I let go of the little repetitive panic attacks of a forest fire where I lived.

Joey is a pro mountain bike racer for Yeti Cycles, a photographer and a lover of mountains. He grew up riding his bike in the woods around our home and immediately after the fire spent numerous hours riding and filming in the burn zone. His 2010 bio for Yeti is a hauntingly beautiful film of the land after the fire from the eyes of a biker. Whether this was therapeutic or not, I cannot say. He did suffer from some nasty PTSD and was eventually helped by a wonderful therapist in Boulder who I saw as well.

Melvina, born at home in these mountains, is trained as a lawyer. She flew from New York the day after the fire and stayed with us until we were settled with friends and our insurance claim was well underway. Her skills as a legal negotiator were invaluable in navigating the insurance morass and her caretaking, loving nature was wonderfully soothing.

The fire was swift and definitive. There was probably only a half an hour from the time we smelled smoke until we had to pack up and leave. Ours was one of the first houses to burn. The wind was intense and was swirling around in all directions. Cinders blew over gulches and spread the fire quickly to many unlikely areas. It was the insistence of our son that made us realize it was time to go.

I was having trouble making the leap from not wanting to have to put everything back if it was only a "fire drill" to the reality of losing everything I didn't take right then. As we were leaving we could see our neighbor's house go up in flames and knew we were next. There was no doubt. I called our insurance agent on the way down the mountain. We went to our office in town and began the "process."

When Melvina arrived, we immediately began the insurance claim. She took charge and helped with the initial adjuster meetings and gave us tasks to itemize our home contents. Right before we fled, my husband had directed our son to open every drawer and door and photograph everything in the house. I had also grabbed a few bags of photographs. Melvina then prepared a ninety-five page document with photos and pricing that she directed us to research. With her help, and the help of our agent and adjuster, we were given the full amount insurance could provide us. This piece was handled. Next were the hearts and bodies.

In the first few weeks, my sister flew out from Oregon and took me to a yoga retreat in Estes Park. We stayed in a cabin on a lake that my husband and I had designed (me as an interior designer and him as an architect) and which was graciously offered to us. The yoga retreat was a little overwhelming for me due to the number of people, but staying at the cabin was divine. I sat by the lake on the warm grass with my feet in the water, praying for my connection through the earth to my old home to continue—and to create a new connection. I asked the earth to hold me. This was a prayer I came back to often in our search for a new home and still find solace in.

So many friends and clients offered us places to stay during that time. We ended up in the basement apartment of friends we worked with for many years. Our son was a block away with good friends we had also worked with for years. Being surrounded by warm friendship and familiarity was a blessing. It was from this place of comfort that we began to try to find a place to live while we put our lives back together.

The community of Boulder immediately opened its heart to all of the fire victims. There were wonderful dinners provided by the very best restaurants in town. Local merchants discounted anything we might need, and the healing arts and yoga practitioners all offered us their services. A "free" store was set up with community donations of furniture, clothing, books, etc. It all created the profound effect of being cared for that absolutely promoted healing and gratitude.

Our lives began to be influenced by a series of miracles. By chance, the house next door to our friends where our son was staying came on the rental market. The current renters had to break their lease and return to Europe, and two days later we had a home in a familiar and comfortable neighborhood. It was a wonderful and healing ten months living close to people who cared for us and fed us constantly. A wonderful therapist that we all loved supported us as well.

It was never an option for us to return to the mountains to rebuild. We toyed with the idea of a summer cabin but it became clear we all wanted to be in town even though we had some "mountain-y" requirements. We wanted quiet, dark nights, and to be surrounded by nature. And, even more important, a nearby fire hydrant. I continually prayed for the universe to provide and for my connection with the earth to be maintained.

Over the next six months we searched for a home to buy in Boulder. Everything was too expensive or too close to noisy students or traffic. Nothing was quite right. We were clear on what we needed but began to despair of finding anywhere to live. One day we walked up onto the porch of a small historic bungalow nestled in the trees up against the side of the mountain under Flagstaff. The key didn't fit in the door, but without going inside, I was sure this was where I wanted to live.

The miracles that happened in rapid succession from this day until we moved into that small house are too numerous to mention. My amazingly talented husband created a home for my son and me that we never cease to be amazed by. We all love, love, love our new home. I felt held and cared for in this magical space. Everyone who helped to make this a home seemed to bring all of their positive energy and best talents. They were people we both worked with for many years, and the generosity of their involvement was a delight.

I had broken my hip about a month before we bought the house. A word of caution, stress will quickly deplete your bone density. Consequently, my husband, son, and helpers did the heavy lifting. My son and his friends went up to our old home site on Melvina Hill and salvaged whatever they could. They brought down all the sandstone pavers that created the patios. New patios were laid here at the house, and they made wonderful outdoor spaces.

My husband made many trips back up the mountain and transplanted flowers and bushes that survived the fire. Our new home now incorporates elements of the old. It is quiet, dark at night, and surrounded by beautiful eighty-year-old trees and the mountains. I have never returned to Melvina Hill since the first few times. I have been busy loving my new home and feeling cared for by the universe.

The most precious gift of the many I was given during this period of time is the incredible closeness that developed in our family. We are survivors, grounded together in love and trust in the benevolence of the universe. And we have a fire hydrant at the end of our driveway.

No Ordinary Fire

Sandi Yukman

A t noon on June 23, 2012, I was called to report to the Safeway on Colorado Avenue and 31st Street in Colorado Springs. As a firefighter, I had been dispatched to many fires over the years and know that being dispatched does not always mean a team will be placed on the fire. So, I reported but half expected to be home in time for dinner. I watched the plume of smoke rise from Waldo Canyon as I drove toward the staging area and knew this was different. Getting my gear ready, I shook as I laced up my fire boots. This was no ordinary fire.

While listening to my radio, I learned that we would indeed be headed to the fire. I double-checked my gear to make sure I was prepared. I had to try and keep my pack as light as possible. While I had trained to carry a 45 lb. pack, I knew I would be more effective with a lighter pack. It is always a trade-off for me because I am 5' 1", 100 lbs., and am more challenged carrying the really heavy gear, like chainsaws, into fires. My wildland fire team members never expected any less from me because of my size, so I had to be in tip top shape and always prepared!

As we drove toward the smoke, I still didn't feel afraid. It seemed so far away. In fact, for the first three days, it *was* fairly far away. I served as a watch-out for much of that time. I spun weather and called temperatures, humidity levels, wind strength, and direction into the Incident Command Center every hour. Everyday temperatures were in the upper 90's. After the first day, I developed a heat rash from head to toe. I used Desitin to stop the itching. While I smelled like a baby's butt, I was able to get through the next few days of heat and sweat.

At other times during the day, I cleared wood and propane tanks from homes in the Cedar Springs neighborhood. At the end of each day, we reported back to staging at Coronado High School. The community was amazing and provided us with food, drink, socks, baby powder, and anything else we needed. One evening, while reporting in before being released for the day, we drove in and saw piles of bottled water. The most wonderful thing for a firefighter after a day of hot weather work is a cold bottle of water. We wore Nomex, which is fire resistant but very hot!

While we had plenty of water, it was nowhere near cold enough! I walked over to the small plastic swimming pool full of ice to get a cold bottle of water. There was a little girl about six years old putting water bottles into the pools. I will never forget the look she gave me. It was one of surprise and delight. She turned to her dad and said, "You mean they make girl firefighters?!" I smiled at her and thanked her. Suddenly, she ran over to her dad. He bent down to listen to her and then looked at me and said, "She wants to give you a hug." It was the best hug I have every gotten. It made me realize that I could and would do this for as many days as it took to beat this fire.

On Tuesday, June 26, I was again spinning weather and watching the fire move. We had set approximately ten trigger points, scenarios that would indicate the fire is moving into a position where we are no longer safe in our current location. As the heat rose and the afternoon rolled around, fire activity picked up and all of our trigger points occurred within forty-five minutes. It was then that my engine partner and I were forced to "bug out," leaving our post to rejoin our team.

I was so happy to see my team again as we gathered at Centennial and 30th. We listened to our radios and found that the fire had indeed come into the city. There were hundreds of firefighters waiting to go in as 32,000 evacuated people were rushing to get out. It was at this point that I felt an unbelievable sense of urgency. We had to get in there right away! Why were they not sending us in?

I became extremely anxious, not because I feared for my life but because I feared we would lose a home. We had been able to keep the fire from homes for the past three days, and I was afraid of failing to do this for those in the Mountain Shadows neighborhood.

It seemed to take forever to get an assignment to go in and start protecting homes, but I was shocked what we drove in to—a firestorm. We were asked to work a cul-de-sac with twenty-two homes. The cul-de-sac had a fire hydrant at the end of the block. Our task force leader told us to "take thirty seconds and assess whether you can make a difference on the house; if not, move onto the next one." Driving in, there were so many homes fully engulfed in flame, it didn't even take thirty seconds to make the decisions. Two of them were completely engulfed as we drove in, and two were completely gone by the time we got there.

I have never seen so much fire in all directions. It was eerily dark, but the sun was still out. The smoke was so thick I had to use a bandana over my mouth to breathe. I remained calm only because my squad boss took control and gave us all our assignments. I worked beside my team members to haul the hoses out and try to put the fires out.

At one point, we stood in the driveway of a fully engulfed home spraying water on the chimney of the house next door when the entire garage door fell over, almost on top of us. Scared and surprised, we regrouped and hit the chimney from a different location. By this time, it was literally raining embers. I remember my squad boss telling us to be sure and put every ember out. I thought to myself "there is no way!" So, although not the most efficient decision, I started to just stomp out the embers. They fell faster than I could even hope to get them out. At that point, I picked up a garden hose and put out a swing set and the burning landscape around the house. I wish I could say that was the best use of my skills but it was clear that the chaos around me was affecting my concentration.

At one point, I was put on hydrant duty. On hydrant duty, I was responsible for hooking up the hose to the hydrant to refill the engines holding 350–500 gallons. Now I knew that when the hydrant valve is turned left, water does not flow. When the valve is turned right, water flows. We were refilling one of the tanks and as the engine's tank started to overflow, I turned the valve right and soaked my fellow firefighter. I was completely concentrating and still made mistakes.

My next assignment was to head behind a home with a hand tool and put out smoldering plants behind a house we saved. The hillside was really steep, and I kept sliding down. It took a while but we got the hillside vegetation out. I remember looking behind me and seeing fire as far as I could see! I said to my firefighting buddy, "We are never going to get all these fires out." It was such a helpless feeling!

Several times, we conducted a personnel accountability report (PAR) to ensure everyone was okay. During one PAR, one of our teammates was missing. That is the only time I truly felt panicked. I started to yell his name at the top of my lungs. This was totally ineffective because the wind was blowing so hard and the engine pumps were so loud, you could not hear anything except for the propane tanks exploding in the garages.

It felt like forever, but it was probably only ten seconds until my firefighting team member emerged from behind a home. I realized then that these guys around me were what really mattered. They were there to protect me, and I was there to protect them. I kept a close eye and counted our team members every five minutes after that scare.

We were in the cul-de-sac for seven hours and it felt like one hour. I remember not feeling hungry and not having to use the bathroom the entire time. That just meant I was not drinking enough. I honestly felt like I didn't have time to drink. After all, people were losing their homes!

When we were finally released and asked to head back to the staging area, I was relieved but reluctant to leave. You see, we still had homes on fire all over the city and we knew we had lost some. I remember eating a small bag of chips at the staging area and feeling kind of in shock. Other firefighters were waiting to go in and replace us. I wasn't tired, just sad.

I can truly say I felt like we had failed our city. How could we have let that fire into our city? Why hadn't we stopped it? Had everyone gotten out safely?

I drove home in tears. What had just happened? I got home around 1:30 am. My husband was asleep so I was unable to decompress by talking about what I had just seen, so I showered and went to bed.

I slept very little that night and could not wait to get back to the fire. I had to do an interview with several news reporters very early before the morning briefing and did so in a bit of a haze. I had trouble keeping my composure as I spoke. I was so emotional! Why could I not keep it together? I didn't want to be away from my team and could not wait to join them. I was so happy to get back with them and head back into the area to continue fighting the fire.

The fire made another run that next day, but we were able to keep it from entering the Peregrine Neighborhood. We had success that day but it didn't seem to make up for the previous night.

Eventually all the fires were out and the sun reappeared. What we saw was horrific! There were so many dead animals (deer and wild turkeys). Devastation like I'd never seen. I felt like 9/11 had happened all over again, only this time it was in my community! Two people also lost their lives that night, and four of the 356 homes lost were in the cul-de-sac we were supposed to protect.

For weeks and months after the fire, I felt like I had let down the community. We should have stopped that fire, and instead, many of my friends had lost everything! I personally knew several people who lost their homes. It was a feeling that was hard to shake. Even as people held up signs thanking us up and down the streets, I felt bad about the fire.

I guess, as a firefighter, I'll never be satisfied if someone loses their life or life-long possessions and home, but it gets easier as the community rebuilds and rebounds. June 23 is a night that changed my life, and I will never forget it.

My Paradise

Louise Creager

This morning as I drove up the mile from our apartment to our newly built home, I was thinking about writing. When I arrived I sat myself down in a chair in our new bedroom with its newly textured walls, and looked out over the horizon. It snowed this past weekend and from our metal roof the snow is jutting off, yet still clinging for dear life. Icicles blown by the wind extend outward, and then curve back toward the house like claws from an enormous eagle.

A beautiful white blanket covers the horizon and the felled, blackened trees. Over behind the house, big puffy cotton balls of snow hang in the branches of remaining, standing trees. The sun is saying it's good morning to the world and our dog Ruby, who has seen fire and rain, is always at our side.

My original intent was to share our experience with the "Evil Insurance Empire" who took our list of possessions, from toothpicks to toothbrushes, and turned them into a garage sale table of items with price tags reading as though they are trash; our treasures, with one word—DEPRECIATION. I decided it would have to serve in another book, another chapter! There are many happy stories to share from our experience and I would rather these be my legacy.

From the initial evacuation at 3:00 PM on June 9, 2012, it seemed people were waiting to be special angels. The manager of my real estate firm had just walked in the door where I was holding an open house. As I was packing up to leave, my phone rang. I answered and heard what would become a familiar notification over the next few weeks to thousands of folks in the foothills west of Fort Collins. "You have two hours to evacuate" is all I remember.

My manager was one of the first to offer his assistance, and was an important source of support during this time, but despite the growing gray and black clouds off toward the foothills, I felt confident that the gathering crews of firefighters would stamp out the fire in due time. Besides, the fire was over six miles away, as the crow flies, from our house, I didn't have the feeling this was to be the "Big One" we've talked about over the years that we knew was coming.

Arriving home, my husband BJ had already removed many items he felt were important for us to preserve. I called our roommate, a friend who had been staying with us between jobs, to ask what she would want—of course her precious cat, and some miscellaneous personal possessions. After packing our own personal items, we were ready to make our way down the mountain, allowing the park ranger to tag our home—"Vacant."

On the way down the canyon, as soon as our phone was in range, it rang. It was our best friend, our next angel, calling to see if we had evacuated. When I answered that we had, she insisted we stay with her at her home in Wellington. We gratefully accepted. It takes a special person to accept three displaced humans, two cats, and a dog, as they descend upon your quiet home where you live with your own animals. She had already planned our dinner and had moved her own possessions to the basement to make room for what was to become our new space for re-growing our lives.

On Tuesday, June 12, at 9:03, one of the firefighters, also a friend, called us. I don't envy this task for anyone. I could only imagine the pain in battling fire to protect the neighbors you have special friendships with, who your children grew up with—and then to have to tell them the beast has won. He told me that it had been impossible to save our home.

Despite our efforts to do all the things we had learned (creating defensible space, keeping grasses around the house short, trimming ladder fuels) the flames that towered 200 feet over our house, and rushed toward the firefighters at forty miles an hour, had won. It didn't matter that our house was built of insulated concrete forms, was protected by metal siding and a metal roof. The flames still won. We are grateful that none of the firefighters were seriously harmed.

A few minutes after I learned that our beautiful home that my husband had built was gone another friend called. She too had been evacuated and was calling to check on us. Fortunately their home had been spared. After our conversation, I discovered she informed the world of our news via Facebook. Within minutes, we began receiving phone calls. Facebook brought invitations to us for homes of people to stay with them, or saying they would be on vacation and we could stay in their homes.

A friend who owns a consignment store set up a special evening where many ladies brought clothes, shoes, as well as other special needs for me personally. I suddenly had a new wardrobe to choose from. Over a dozen large bags of clothes were all mine for the choosing. Some still had tags on them. After going through these in the days to come, and choosing which new treasures would fit and go together, I returned the rest. The clothes continued their journey to Colorado Springs where my friend's mother almost lost her home in the Waldo Canyon fire.

To one of my special friends, I mentioned I no longer had any crosses. She posted on Facebook I'd lost my cross collection. Before it wasn't a "collection," but it certainly is now! One generous woman gave me the pendant her husband had given her for an anniversary. When I tried to object, she insisted that he was thrilled she was sharing this special gift with me. These crosses all have their own home above my desk and are a daily reminder of the love that was shared with me.

As a real estate professional, every day I meet wonderful people. A client called one day and said he had just bought a new car and wanted to give his old Jeep to someone who had lost their vehicle in the fire. I knew exactly who that should be. One of the firefighters, who lost his home, his tools for his livelihood, his truck, car, and a couple of motorcycles, no longer had a means to make his living. Folks from all around the neighborhood donated extra tools from their personal collections, and even bought him some. A prior customer of his, and some friends, bought him an Airstream to live in.

It was perfect timing; we met over at this lovely gentleman's home, and you could tell from the very bright smile he wore how thrilled he was to be passing on his car to our firefighter, who in turn was so grateful to receive this gift. I just saw him this week, and he regaled me with fun stories of his exploits with the car.

Every once in a while little blessings occur that can only be explained by saying my angels are watching out for me. One day, I was particularly despondent. It seemed everything with rebuilding the house was going wrong. I was having difficulties in my business, my husband and I were at each other, and the insurance company was pestering us to get the never-ending inventory list done. I just wanted to scream (and did in the confines of my car!).

Later that day, my very best friend called to invite me to lunch. Then a card came in the mail from my daughter— just to say how much she was so happy to have me as her mother. That very same evening my son called to see if we could have dinner. And my husband did all the dishes when I arrived at our apartment. I said a very grateful prayer that night, thanking my angels and God for taking the blues from me, and fell asleep knowing that we are not alone in this journey. While not all sad days end up this way, it was a nice reminder not to let sadness get the better of me.

In November 2013, I had a very hard time when I thought about Christmas. We were living at a friend's one bedroom apartment above her shop. Nice and cozy, but there would be no room for our children to visit us. That was a particularly hard time. I called my daughter to say I didn't know what to do and just sobbed. I had never done that before and felt I had failed as a parent.

Showing such weakness was not the example I wanted her to see. Suddenly, it occurred to me, we didn't have to stay in the apartment! We could rent a condo in Estes Park. As a bonus, our family agreed it would be nice to support Estes Park after terrible flooding had cut the town off from much of the area.

This will always be one of my favorite holidays. Our children surprised us by bringing up a live tree and decorating it with some of the fun lights we had purchased the year before. Then there were the ornaments—snowmen, Santa, blue dogs, and tiny angels—all scrounged up and snuck in by our son. The live tree was planted that spring next to our new house. It's a daily reminder that with a little inspiration you can turn another day of sadness into a wonderful memory.

Many folks have asked me since the fire—why did you rebuild? Why not move to town? First of all, it is our home where so many wonderful memories had been created, from the designing and building of the house, to our children growing up in a community where my neighbor may live over five miles away, but their family is still considered neighbors and good friends. Everyone looks out for the other in the event of any emergency—even when we have heavy snowfalls. We call each other to make sure we all have what we need in the case we are stranded. I always joke when people ask me if I feel stranded—I say to them, "I *hope* the power goes out so I don't have to work!"

Many of these neighbors are helping us rebuild. Their talents and creativity are building a new home for us, another one to be proud of. Each piece they build will be a new memory that makes this house a special home, becoming a special part of our lives, where all are welcome.

We traditionally held the New Year's Eve party, and in 2014 we were able to host it once again. I look forward to the house being enveloped with music and laughter to fill these granite walls with new wisps of memories. Is my cup half full—or half empty? I say it's overflowing. Already many new warm memories have been created for us. There is not enough space here to thank all the wonderful organizations, stores, and mostly people who have given to us in so many ways. Please accept this as one person saying thank you!

Most folks see deer, wild turkey, foxes, and other critters that allow us to share their home—only in zoos, museums, or books. At home, we have the opportunity of seeing these beautiful creatures regularly, on any given day. I live in Rist Canyon, Colorado—and this is my paradise.

SHADES

BETH CUTTER

My house was here. How strange to reconcile
The home we made, its colors and designs
With what remains: this random shard of tile,
A dozer track, the wind in distant pines.

This lot scraped bare was once my domicile.
To grasp a house was here may take a while
When just beyond what meets the eye I see
Thanksgiving dinners, grace, a sleeping child.
These didn't burn; they were not in the fire.

A backyard ballgame, love, a Christmas tree,
Chaotic birthday party games, a pile
Of grass-stained jerseys; peace once in a while:

These shades shine bright. Although the vagaries
Of wind and white-hot embers blowing wild
Consumed my house, these were not on the pyre.

Some paintings gone, notes, books and jewelry—
Mementos of this life I had acquired.
My house was here—this much I reckon while
I grasp how much endured through fiery trial.

THE 503:
THE THINGS WE
LEAVE BEHIND

MELISSA FRY

T he 503. That's what my husband Evan always called it because we lived at 503 Wild Turkey Trail. You can't get a better mountain address than that, although we'll be the first to admit that living twenty minutes outside of Boulder isn't exactly roughing it in the wilds of Alaska. But The 503, a blue and gray tri-level house, nestled down a dirt road among a shroud of pine trees, too deep in the canyon for rock star views yet tucked in enough to feel like there was no one around for miles, was its own slice of paradise. Birds and bears. Fox and fauna. It was the first time I'd ever "lived up in the mountains."

My husband grew up in rural Oregon, but coming from Louisiana, this was my first taste of Colorado living. And I loved it there. We loved it there. I would walk my beloved black Labrador, Lucas, up the dirt roads to Arkansas peak. Evan would ride his bike to Gold Hill, Lyons, and back.

We celebrated there. Argued there. Hosted friends and family. Enjoyed the mundane and the prolific. It was home. And home is the ultimate escape. And The 503 was that all time. But on the morning of September 6, 2010, Evan and I were having pancakes for breakfast, and by nightfall The 503 was gone.

When people hear that you lost your home in a wildfire, their first reaction is always one of sympathetic horror. There's no debating it. Homeowners, completely innocent. Wildfire, Mother Nature. It's primal. It's alarming to lose our nest, the place where we are supposed to feel our safest and, most optimistically, our happiest.

When destruction comes in the form of something as undiscerning as a wildfire, it humbles and terrifies us. Left to scramble like a colony of ants whose hill has been casually kicked, we are powerless. Months after the fire. Evan and I observed that even if we'd been able to empty out the entire house, the loss of The 503 would likely have been just as devastating.

After hearing about the loss of one's home, the first question people usually ask is "Were you able to get out most of your things?" When asking this question, most people mean sentimental items, photos, heirlooms, personal treasures. If I ever responded "Not really, and I'm pretty sad I lost a beautiful Diane von Furstenberg jacket," the reaction might still have been horror, but doubtfully sympathetic. That's not what you're supposed to say when you lose everything in a natural disaster. We're supposed to, at best, remind ourselves that "It's all just stuff" and focus on the fact that no one was hurt. And at worst, lament irreplaceable mementos.

And I am glad no one was hurt. But we're expected to remember that everything can be replaced and keep moving forward. But mourning the loss of "stuff" is tricky. While it feels, in part, superficial, as humans it is our nature to create, collect, and treasure even the most mundane objects. They are part of who we are. Comfort at the end of a long day. Relics of our past. Evidence of our existence.

The caveat: wildfires are no joke. People lose pets, family members, even their own lives in wildfires; all horrors I cannot bear to imagine. And around the world, human lives are lost in unimaginable ways every minute. On their best day, many people would probably trade places with me on my worst. So while it's an enlightened perspective to keep in mind that worse things do happen, it doesn't change the fact that losing our homes and our belongings is a miserable experience.

So whenever I have friends who are debating evacuating their home with the threat of an oncoming wildfire (not an uncommon occurrence in Colorado), I tell them, don't just grab items that have sentimental value, as these are easy to rationalize. But also grab items that provide comfort, like the worn out T-shirt you've had since college or the ugly brown mug that you love for your morning coffee. Or even that designer Diane von Furstenberg jacket.

And most importantly, do not waste time judging what those things are. They are a part of you and you will need their comfort in a crisis. If after you've made it to safety you feel you need to reassess your values, fine. But in the moment, just go for it.

On the morning of the fire, we were sitting down at the kitchen table when we noticed that very distinct smell of a wildfire—acres of trees burning en masse. It is a smell you will always recognize. The smell of fresh flame and heat turning sap, leaves, and wood into cinders, charcoal, and ash. As we looked out the window, smoke began to fill the sky creating a surreal orange haze. We knew there must be a fire somewhere, so Evan headed out in his truck to find out what was happening. As I walked through the house, unsure of what I should be doing, the power suddenly died and a reverse 911 call came ordering us to evacuate.

After hanging up the phone, I went straight to our closet. I remember standing there with an open suitcase, Lucas staring quizzically up at me, and thinking "This is crazy! What am I supposed to do?" It felt overly dramatic to start grabbing more than just a couple of days' worth of clothes. And it certainly felt superficial to grab anything not practical or highly sentimental. No one grabs bathing suits when evacuating a home. I recall opening a closet door, staring at a handbag, then immediately shutting the door, leaving it there, ashamed because I was sure I was more evolved than that.

The process of deciding what to take felt like a moral test, with the implicit questions: "What *really* matters to me? What are my priorities?" I wanted to pass that test. So I went around the house and looked at other items, books from India, my stash of cozy winter scarves, an artist's photograph of a vulture I'd given to Evan. But I decided to leave those things.

I even decided not to change the clothes I was wearing for something I liked more. It was a mix of confusion and self-doubt for wanting to rescue "things." But I think moreover I was also telling myself, "If you don't go for the big things, it won't happen."

Evan returned with the news that he and some neighbors had met on a ridge. They could see it coming, a fiery neon-orange wave cresting over the next canyon, lapping the sky with black smoke. As we hurried around the house we looked at items and looked back at each other as if to say, "Are we supposed to take this?" Ultimately we decided to "think good thoughts" and plan for the best. So we grabbed a couple days' worth of clothes, passports, and photo albums. It was as if taking more than that would be bad luck.

Before we left, we sat on the deck looking toward a strand of Tibetan prayer flags we'd hung between two pine trees and shared a toast of Wild

Turkey. "To The 503!" Before leaving, Evan patted a wall of the house and said, "Don't worry, friend, we'll be back."

We went to a friend's house and as a light rain of ash began to fall over Boulder, we hoped all day that our home would be spared. I can only describe this time, waiting to know what's happened, as surreal. A part of you who wants to think positive and believe everything will be fine. Another part of you tries to go ahead and prepare yourself for the worst. Even then, the thought of items I'd left behind began to creep in and I remember thinking "Why did I wear *these* sandals? I don't even like them. But at least the vacuum happened to be in the car."

The mind has an odd way of grappling with impending doom. Trying to quickly right itself when the current wants to pull it over the falls, it will grasp for any rock or branch, no matter how absurd.

Later that night, wanting to move our anxiety away from well-meaning friends, we found ourselves at The Kitchen, a local Boulder hang out. Over dinner, a neighbor called Evan. He'd ridden his motorcycle up our dirt road and confirmed it was all gone. Oscillating between numbing grief and manic denial, we tried to convince ourselves "Oh well!" Half drunk on red wine. "Oh well." Our neighbor may as well have told us that Martians had taken the house.

I'd rather lose everything in a fire than a flood. The choice is made for you. There's something supernatural, almost holy, about everything incinerating into infinity versus the trauma of sorting through ruined and water-logged treasures, grappling with whether or not to try to save them. I know this to be true because I moved to Colorado from New Orleans after Hurricane Katrina. Compared to most folks, I did fine. But I had many friends whose homes were destroyed. Friends who were left digging thru soggy rubble, the walls of their homes infested with mold well beyond the water line, their children's toys crushed, family photos inky and warped. But essentially most of their belongings were still there, leaving the agonizing decision of what to save and what to throw away.

My husband bought The 503 while we were dating. And, while I spent most of my time there with him before finally moving in a few weeks before the fire, it was the first house he'd ever purchased that was truly his home. I remember the day we first saw it. "This is it," he said smiling. It was the weekend of his birthday, and after working years to build a successful career, he'd saved up the money and bought it. An intimate sanctuary quietly nestled within the pine trees, providing the privacy he loved so much.

So when the county finally allowed residents to return, he went up first, alone. I remember him calling me at work in tears of disbelief. "It's all gone. There's nothing left," was all he could say. The next day, we both went there, and I couldn't believe what I was—or wasn't—seeing.

The idea of a burned down house had always conjured up images of a scorched, but still recognizable, structure: a smoldering frame standing in pieces, perhaps a blackened, still-smoking sofa in its usual place near the fireplace. All charred, but there, just under a layer of ash that one could wipe away and still find home. But that's not how the inferno of wildfires works. Our 3400-square-foot home had been reduced to a pool of sandy ash.

There was some recognizable debris. Cement walls that once framed the walkout basement now encompassed a filthy beach. Rows of nails lay on the ground in perfect alignment where the wood and glass they were once attached to had violently evaporated. A huge steel I-beam lay across the debris, mangled like a straw someone had mindlessly twisted into a knot and left on a table. But other things I thought I'd see, the three-story staircase, major appliances, the outline of our chimney—it was as if they had never existed.

Oddly enough, what did show grit was pottery. Fine, delicate things that only fire can create, so it cannot destroy. There were plates, cups, and other items that suffered too many breaks and fiery poisons to be used again, but had survived in pieces. So I fished out some things: a tiny blue creamer I loved because, well, it was tiny and blue. A cast iron skillet we had used for making cornbread. Evan pulled out pieces of the house's bones. Joists and steel.

But amidst it all, a piece of light green Peruvian pottery that had sat on a dresser on the third floor remained totally intact. I imagined it, enduring the scorching oven enveloping our home, floating down and landing safely on the heap of ash where we found it, aside from some slight scorching, not a crack, not a chip. It reminds me that strength and resilience can abide in the most delicate of packages, and it sits on its own shelf in our home today.

Another unexpected survivor was the strand of Tibetan prayer flags hanging perfectly intact between two blackened pine trees. Astonishing. A sign? Or maybe an answer to whether or not we could survive this. Rebuild here? Stay? Evan kept those flags close to him for a long time after the fire. They were with us until my beloved Lucas, who had evacuated with us, passed away three years later. We laid them with him as he fell into his final sleep. And with him, they too eventually disappeared into the fire of cremation.

In that house was a lifetime of "things" gone. Sentimental to superficial and I had to allow myself to grieve losing them all. A beautiful, but modest, collection of scarves I'd bought traveling alone in northern India. An old thrift store Saints T-shirt that reminded me of the humid summers in New Orleans. The Diane von Furstenberg jacket that I simply loved wearing, because it looked good and felt great. Eames chairs I'd found at a garage sale. And so if they were just things, they should have been easy to replace.

I was blessed to have good insurance, so when I received a check to replace much of what I lost, I found it wasn't as easy (or exciting) as I had envisioned. Upon entering an upscale department store, I realized they hardly had anything I wanted. They didn't have the cool old coat I'd scored at a thrift store for $9, or the silver necklace, a choker set with moonstone, my grandfather had given my grandmother—his first gift to her. They did not stock the collection of matchbox cars that belonged to Evan's brother, Eric, who had sadly passed away when they were young.

While it is a blessing and a relief to have access to funds to replace expensive and necessary items, to gather up new and beautiful things, they're all new. They're nice to have, but initially, they're imposters. They have no history or story. They haven't packed up and moved with you. Been part of the adventure.

We are still us without these things, and their loss teaches us so much about who we are, but their memories are strong. They represent more than the money spent or the effort made to acquire them. They are remnants of entire eras, of family and friends, things we'd accomplished, and journeys we'd made. Sadness and celebrations. Loss and victory. They are the residue of our journey.

And so while these things don't provide ultimate meaning or purpose, they do provide context and comfort. They outline who we are because we have chosen them, been given them. And we are complex creatures who have an inherent need to curate these things that become props in the happening that is our lives. And so, it is an odd process of grief and acceptance when we lose, miss, and try to replace them.

As I said, losing home is primal. It's the place we go to exhale during crisis. And when the crisis is that *home* is gone, that safety net has been ripped away. My husband was bound to our home. It was his quiet retreat. He felt such a connection to it that he struggled with a gnawing sense of guilt for not staying behind to protect it, regretting that something that had given us so much comfort was left to burn alone.

But all of the things we lost there—sentimental or superficial—were remnants of ourselves. And, like the house, they too were helplessly left behind to burn alone. We miss those "things" as much as we miss our home. But looking back and understanding our profound connection to those things, memories incarnate, I realize now that The 503 didn't burn alone. We were there. We were with it.

STARTING OVER

JACKIE KLAUSMEYER

One week shy of my fifty-ninth birthday and all I feel is old. Maybe that's the influenza talking. Actually, I *know* it's the influenza talking. I've been marooned on this island called "Bed" since Tuesday night. It's Saturday now and I can comfortably say that, while I no longer fear death from the cellular takeover of my body by an army of mucous-carrying, bomb-shaped invaders, I am nowhere near back to normal. In fact, I almost forget what normal feels like.

I *will* say this: being sick sure does give a person time to reflect. It seems as if the past few months all I've done is complain. Complain about the mud. Complain about small spaces. Complain about how *long* it takes to build a house. I mean, think about it; compared to say, breathing, how important *is* it that this is the muddiest spring here on the mountain in probably twenty-five years?

What's *wrong* with a few more dirt clods in The Barge, anyway? Nobody ever said living in a 30 foot travel trailer would be anything but camping. At least the dirt outside is diggable (yep, kind of important when you're building a house), The Barge keeps us warm and dry, and the drought (for now anyway) is a not so pleasant, distant memory.

Stack up those annoyances against an expensive room in the hospital, and I guess what you have is "perspective." A room at the hospital might not be muddy, but clearly it's no place to hang your hat. The Barge might not be home, but it works just fine and is *not* a room in the local hospital. Hmmm… maybe this flu bug showed up just in the nick of time. Clearly, my attitude was due for an adjusting.

After the fire, our friends told my husband that, as a couple, we were like poster children for how people who lost everything should move forward in the aftermath of a disaster. Was it because we truly saw "The Big One" coming and, in some strange way, were actually relieved when it finally happened? (YEAH! The Fire Monster came, went, and didn't kill us!) Probably, there's some truth there. I *can* say that looking back on the days of drought and tinder dry, "beetle kill" trees taking over our forests, leaving brown, fuel-loaded trees in their wake, I had become fearful and reluctant to even *leave home* without being sure someone *at all times* stayed behind, prepared to evacuate. The drought made me deeply, intrinsically nervous. I casually mentioned to a few different people—my vet, my boss, my mother—that I had never been afraid of living in the mountains, until the drought moved in and would not leave.

Do bears scare me? Absolutely not! Do mountain lions scare me? A little, but more for my horses than for myself. (And, I keep reminding *them* that God gave horses the ability to kick for a good reason!) Do coyotes scare me? Nope, although I certainly don't encourage my dogs to go off and play with them. Does wildfire scare me? Yes, it absolutely does.

My husband and I had an evacuation plan, and we were forced to practice it numerous times; it was as if we warmed up for the "The Big One" by practicing on all the "little" fires first— the ones that blew over, around or beyond us. Those fires belonged to other people, and took other people's lives. Yet, each time we knew it could have been us: our life, our home, our neighborhood.

Looking back, our evacuation drills were clearly time well spent. First, load up two of our trucks with every file drawer out of the office, then throw computers and electronics on top. Next, round up clothing, photographs, and precious items. Load up the five nervous ducks next. Then hitch up the horse trailer, and have the horses standing by, ready to jump in. At that point, we'd be putting our two dogs into the back of one of the pickups, and we'd make one final sweep, looking for treasures and essentials easily overlooked.

We both knew, once the horses were loaded, it would be time to go. And that hot, smoky Saturday afternoon in June of 2012 we weren't hanging out, waiting to see what direction the High Park fire might take. The smoke was menacingly dark, directly overhead, and we knew it was time. We were among the first residents of our canyon to leave the mountain that day; no one needed to call with an evacuation order to report the obvious. This fire was bearing down and moving like a freight train. The sensible person's job was to get out of the freight train's way. We had seen enough of fire to know this one was gonna be a doozy.

I remember coming back to our land for the first time after the fire. Our little community was ravaged. Driving the seven miles up the canyon, then the four miles back in to our place, I remember thinking how random the destruction seemed. We passed one house standing; then one house burned. To the right, sections of forest stood unharmed; to the left, entire swaths of charred mountainside. There was no logic to the destruction (although in retrospect I believe Mother Nature's logic was to be rid of dead trees). In the weeks since I had hung my white bath towel on the front door, signifying to firefighters that no one was home and the people who lived there were safely evacuated, I hadn't given much thought to bracing myself for what I was about to see.

Randy maintained a running commentary as we drove the dirt road approaching home. I remember feeling annoyed at the dialog, but then again, the seemingly never-ending media coverage and repetition of one story after another had begun to take its toll on my good nature. I was sick of talk, sick of the television, sick of the justifications people gave for why "my house survived"—compared to, say, the guy's next door. I was sick of the smoke that hung over everything and sick of the angry dude at the town hall meeting who only wanted to drill the rescue officials about *his* place; and "why, dammit, had no one done anything to save *it*?"

Sadly, perhaps, I was *especially* sick of the people who gave God all the credit for saving their home. *"It was like He reached down and put our place in His hands and made the fire go around us! We are so BLESSED!"* they would say. I was tempted to ask why God felt no such need to reach down, swoop in, and put *my* place in His hands; was I not worthy of being *blessed*? I knew I needed to keep those inner comments, well, inner.

For me, all the talk wasn't helping me move forward. I found myself retreating more and more to the boarding stable where my two beloved palominos were safely housed, for now. My blue heeler accompanied me to the barn and we felt happy there. I looked forward to daily visits from two bubbly horse-crazy girls who loved brushing my horses. They were ecstatic when I allowed them to braid every strand of horsehair their little arms could reach. Can you even imagine their joy when I set them on top of first one horse, then the other, and led them around in circles?

These experiences took me back to a simpler time in my life when just sitting, lying, or tearing across a field on the back of a horse was my own girlish idea of "died and gone to heaven." Yes, I let the fire be someone else's problem when I retreated to the barn; a lot of people didn't understand that, and many did not approve, but for me it was the only action I *could* take that felt sane.

Watching one more *BREAKING NEWS STORY* in front of a blaring television set, or sitting one more time among a group of people rehashing the same story for the umpteenth time, was definitely not for me. To this day, the choice I made to draw inward rather than to find strength in numbers keeps me alienated from those who wish my actions had been different. To this day, I maintain it was not a choice, but rather the instinctive way *I* needed to process *my* grief and loss, the likes of which I had never experienced before.

As we approached our driveway, the first thing I noticed was that the handmade sign I had given Randy as a wedding gift still hung on the same pitch pine post. My beautiful sugar maple tree still stood tall and majestic, although singed from the west by the searing heat that had passed through. Our lilac bushes were alive, and the garden was essentially untouched by fire. The red gate that led into our garden was still intact, although having a gate was pointless considering that most of the fencing had burned.

My garden pond was almost empty of water, and I saw the skeletal remains of our koi and goldfish lying at the bank of the pond, snatched up by a raccoon or hungry bear, no doubt. Then I realized "That's it. This is what's left of my life." Everything else was a pile of rubble, ash, and metal. Our log home, gone (amazingly, without even a trace of the mighty logs that once framed it). Our sweet little guest cabin, gone.

The newly finished outdoor bathhouse, replete with treasures from the ocean and painted bright pink, true to its name "the Flamingo Room," gone. My new barn at the top of the hill, gone. Randy's shop, garage, livelihood, gone. Our lives had essentially vanished and in the fire's wake was a mighty mess. I felt, in that moment, completely incapable of cleaning up. Randy took me in his arms and I sobbed.

I was brought up by parents who had lots of favorite sayings, one of which was "When the going gets tough, the tough get going." I think Randy heard that line a lot as a kid too. Dwelling for too long in mind-numbing powerlessness was *not* an option. For us, it quickly became "roll up your sleeves" time. There was so much to be done! Foremost (for me) was to find a place to live. I remember waking one morning at dawn with the impulse to look for a rental.

Since we were temporarily living at my mother-in-law's, I quietly snuck upstairs and got on the Internet. I immediately found an ad for a studio apartment on horse property in the country—it sounded perfect! I ran back downstairs and woke Randy, ecstatic with the news that I had *already* found a place to live! All of us—horses, dogs, ducks, *and* people—would be able to stay together! When the clock finally indicated the hour was appropriate for making calls, I dialed. "I really don't know about *ducks!*" the man on the other end of the line said. I practically begged him to meet us, to reconsider his hesitancy. "They're a lot like chickens!" I said, "Except they swim." He was firm; the deal was a no-go.

My exuberance quickly turned to disappointment as I began to truly absorb the magnitude of how difficult it might be to find a place where we could all live and stay together. How would I ever find a rental where my dogs could run free—not next to, or worse yet, into—traffic? How could I replace the twenty acres of pasture my horses had at home? How could I find a landlord who embraced *ducks?*

We were lucky, though, because by some miracle we found *The Absolutely Perfect Place to Live.* A friend of a friend just happened to have a basement apartment vacant, and her wish was to help someone affected by the fire. Phone calls were made; friendships were formed, and before we knew it, we (all of us!) went to live at a beautiful horse ranch on forty acres, near the bottom of our beloved canyon where we all stayed together as one family—people, horses, ducks, dogs.

This was the miracle: life and friendship had handed us the ability to live day by day, while at the same time sorting through what to do with the rest of our lives. I no longer felt homeless and adrift; I felt purposeful and safe! My guardian angel lived directly above my head, on the upper floor of her two-story house at Rimrock Ranch.

Randy and I immediately became task oriented. He set to the daunting job of cleaning up our property. I went back to teaching so that we could continue to draw a paycheck and fund insurance. Randy filed claims, attempted to record our "Personal Property List" (which I will not speak of here since the complaining I referred to in the first paragraph might come back with a vengeance), and went to our land every day, surveying damage, chopping down black trees, cleaning up and networking with friends and neighbors.

I furnished the apartment, refusing to live without a sense of home. We lived with all the creature comforts one could imagine and sat together (literally in front of a fireplace!) in the evenings, dreaming and scheming about what we would rebuild. The vision of our new house took form in the nurturing environment of this retreat. Randy set up a drafting table in the deepest back bedroom of our basement apartment, and, together, we designed the house we are now building.

The rest of the story is still unfolding. Our time at Rimrock Ranch was up after a year—that's what the insurance company gave us for a rental—so we bought a thirty-foot travel trailer (I am *so* tempted to use the word "vintage" here, but no, frankly, The Barge is just plain old) and, like many other folks in this predicament, we hauled it and our animals back up to our land. The horses knew immediately where they were, and were glad to be home. The ducks lived in the horse trailer while we rebuilt a poultry house. I write from our queen-sized bed in The Barge now. Just last night, Randy and I had the discussion "What will you miss most about leaving The Barge once we are living in our new home?" We came up with a long list of fondnesses and memories.

The plans for our new home—the same ones we drew up in the basement apartment at Rimrock Ranch—are becoming a reality. The going is slow, but I have no doubt that the result will be worth the wait. Monsoon rains of last summer are still working their way down the valley, directly through the path of our new house site. Who would have thought that the same lack of water, which brought on this disaster, would become overabundance in such a short span of time? The digging is easy, but the mud is a bitch. I look forward to the day when all that water will irrigate one gorgeous expanse of grass in front of my gorgeous new house. I can just see the horses grazing in it now.

We take things as they come, mostly because there is just no other choice. And even on a bad day, there's still no place on earth I'd rather be than here. Where the air is cleaner and the water is cooler. Where we still live together as one family. And where the fire danger is pretty much gone, for today.

RISING FROM
THE ASHES

YVETTE TRANTHAM

I remember…the sun shining brightly; its warmth enveloping me. The birds singing a beautiful melody and the breezes gently blowing through my hair.

As a young girl, the mountain was my favorite place to be. I spent every waking hour running through the tall grass, seeking out caves, and learning the names of the flowers. And then, perched on some tall rock, I would close my eyes, and just listen…listen to the sounds. I tried to isolate and identify what each noise was: grasshoppers, bees, birds, or simply grass whispering in the breeze. These moments warmed my soul and gave me hope.

As I grew into a young woman, I loved the mountain more and more, and it gave me strength. I had children of my own. They too treasured the mountain, and it gave them hope. They would spend their days traversing the mountain, finding secluded rocks to sit on, and searching for fields of columbine. We continued this tradition just as my father had before us.

Our cabin on the mountain was full of family treasures. As I walked from room to room, memories would spark of the past generations. I remember the needlepoint chairs my grandmother made. An old-fashioned ice cream maker that sat in the corner, which my grandmother would bring out on hot summer days to make us dessert. Shelves filled with games that my grandfather and I played for hours. Images of wildlife, painted by my mother, lining the walls.

On the west wall hung a banjo that my father had handcrafted and loved to strum as we gathered around the fireplace. Quilts my mother made covered the beds, each one telling a different story. On the table sat a journal my great aunt had kept. Throughout were antiques belonging to our family for generations—each one with its own tale to tell. And outside, a deck encircled the cabin, which we regularly used for morning parades.

The cabin was truly extraordinary. It not only held a special place in our hearts, but it bonded us together as a family.

One tragic day, fire spread over the mountain. My family was safe in Denver but we waited and waited for news of our beloved cabin. We watched reports, hoping for a glimpse of something that would tell us what was happening. We examined websites. But there was no news, so we waited some more.

Eventually news came…our beloved cabin was gone. In that moment, I felt a vast emptiness. My strength left me and I wasn't sure I would remember how to breathe. It had *all* been taken from us. The fire that spread over the mountain consumed our cabin and all we cherished within it. It torched the trees. It annihilated the flowers. It displaced the deer. It destroyed the homes of many animals. It was all gone. I did not know how to go on. What was life without my cabin? What was life without my mountain?

Ash was all that remained. We spent days upon days sifting through the ashes, looking for anything that survived. There was hope that somehow, something had made it. We searched and searched. Our clothes filthy, our faces blackened by soot, while tears streamed down leaving tracks as they fell. The metal roof was twisted and lay in a pile of rubble.

The antique wood-burning kitchen stove rested on its side, after tumbling downhill. Glass melted in a molten heap. Under all the ash were nails and screws that once held our cabin together. All our hope was for naught. Nothing was salvageable …there was absolutely nothing left.

Eventually, we hired a contractor to remove the heap of rubble, leaving the site completely empty. The mountain looked as bare and scarred as my heart felt. Disappointment and emptiness turned to anger.

Then, as we drove away, I saw a site I will never forget. The forest was filled with charred trees—and it was devastating to see. But I looked closer. New grass had begun to grow a vivid green. The color contrast between the charred trees and the green grass was striking. A lone deer lay amidst it all. A still, small voice spoke to my soul. *There was still life on the mountain.*

Even though it was surrounded by destruction, life went on, and I needed to find a way to continue too. I still wondered how I could possibly go on without my treasured cabin. Where would I find new strength? That still, small voice was the voice of God. He was leading me to the only true source of strength. I recalled a verse I had learned as a child.

"The Everlasting God, the LORD, the Creator of the ends of the earth does not become weary or tired… He gives strength to the weary… those who wait upon the LORD will gain new strength; they will mount up with wings like eagles." Isaiah 40:28–31 (NASB)

From that moment on, I sought strength from God. It was through Him that I began to rise from the devastation. And so my journey of restoration began. I gathered hope from a new source—a supernatural source. I stopped looking inward, and looked outward toward others that were hurting. I saw teen girls that came from difficult families with situations that broke my heart. They did not have love and they did not have hope.

I began to share the love that had been modeled for me by the previous generations of my family. Most importantly, I learned how to listen to others in the midst of grieving, encourage others that they are loved, and inspire others to search out the true source of strength.

This restoration journey has brought good days and bad. Something will spark a sad memory of what was destroyed. My friends' posts on Facebook of their old photos cause me to stop and reflect. Glimpses of needlepoint chairs remind me of the dining room chairs my grandmother lovingly made. An unexpected whiff of fire brings my entire family to tears in an instant.

Those who lost homes and loved ones in the Lower North Fork fire banded together to create a support group. Just as I experienced, these people had both good days and bad. Guest speakers came to our meetings and assisted us through difficult legal matters. The surrounding community offered our group tangible items, such as socks and blankets. We were able to share our anger and our frustration, as well as our encouragement. Because we were all experiencing the same emotions, this group has been an invaluable part of my journey.

Approximately forty trees were donated to us, some large and some just seedlings. We gathered a crew of friends and family and had a tree planting party. They spent hours digging deep into the rocky soil. At the point of exhaustion, we sat on large logs that were felled as a result of the fire. In the quiet of the moment, we heard faint chirping. In one of the newly planted trees sat a nest.

Three baby birds had miraculously made the journey, in their nest, across town and up the mountain. Although we knew we had to assist these chicks who had been separated from the mother, it was another symbol of the wonder of life; another reminder that if you look close enough, you will find miracles.

A year after the fire, we began to rebuild. Now, a new home stands on the mountain. It is bigger and nicer in every way. And yet, the rooms are empty of those memories that once filled the cabin. Some things can never be replaced. My own personal memoirs are lost forever. I can never replace my wedding dress or my baby photos. And yet, I am determined to find a way to fill the home with new memories—ones that can be passed down to my children and their children. We will build beauty from ashes.

THE DREAM

JENN NOLTE

My husband and I had always dreamed of building our own house. It was the encouragement from strangers on a solar home tour that gave us the confidence to move forward with our dream. In 2003, Joel and I purchased a ten-acre lot in the foothills near Fort Collins, Colorado. Time passed as we thinned the heavily treed property and dug out some semblance of a driveway while we saved money to build our home.

In order to decrease building costs, we were always on the lookout for leftover construction materials from previous projects and one-of-a-kind items to incorporate into the design of our home. We kept adding to our growing garage full of windows, specialty tiles, and other unique things as we waited.

When the day came to start building in the fall of 2010, it was the beginning of excitement along with a bit of nervousness. It had been ten long years of saving, living in cheap apartments, and driving old cars. The foundation had been excavated and Joel had ferried load after load of concrete block in our trusty F350. As the Colorado winter set in, we celebrated week after week as Joel got faster at laying the block foundation and hand mixing concrete in a wheelbarrow. A chemist by trade, Joel had put in countless hours of research and consultations with builder friends to learn the various skills building a house required.

In late spring, a local timber framing company erected a gorgeous Colorado White Fir timber frame that stood majestically beside the tall ponderosa pines that dotted our land. The frame raising was a two-day affair complete with one of the biggest cranes I had ever seen.

The smell of fresh cut wood filled the air, and we watched as the talented crew fit posts and beams together via various cuts and notches. As they pounded oak pegs through the joints where wood met wood, friends gathered to watch and celebrate the milestone. That day will always hold a special place in my heart. It meant this was really happening, that waiting had been the right choice, and that the end result would be amazing.

We hired friends who were plumbers, radiant heat specialists, and electricians. Not only did we want experts who took pride in their work, but this project was sacred to us and we didn't want just anyone working on it. As 2012 rolled around, the drywall was ready for painting, the hand-poured concrete floors were ready for stain, and the soaking tub that would fit under a skylight in our master bathroom had arrived. The salvaged decorative tiles with aspen leaves that I had found were incorporated nicely into the tile work in the guest shower.

Joel had laid the last piece in the natural stone veneer on the two-story chimney. The trim carpenters had been hard at work installing the beautiful alder baseboards and window trim as part of the final details. The glass jar lights with Edison bulbs were hanging on either side of the sink, and Joel and I would turn on the lights in the evening, run outside, and stand in awe. Joel and I had hand-stained the concrete floors a deep reddish orange. The pale straw color of the wooden beams contrasted nicely with the floor, and the beetle kill tongue and groove ceiling picked up the bluish hues in the stonework on the chimney.

The eyebrow window that we had found brought in light for the office space in the loft. The black iron railings framed the oak treads on the steps going up to the loft and master bedroom. All the hours spent poring over color samples of every material imaginable, different species of wood, and placement of shelving had been worth it. The house was coming together beautifully, just as I had hoped.

I spent hours just staring at various aspects of the house, unable to imagine that it was really going to be ours. I had never decorated any of the rentals we had lived in since we were going to move again anyway. I couldn't wait to hang pictures on walls without worrying about getting charged for the nail holes! All our furniture had been hand-me-downs from family or friends, and I relished the idea of putting a home together that was esthetically pleasing as well as comfortable and inviting. At the age of thirty-nine, I was more than ready to finally have a place to call home.

I was driving up to the house on June 9, 2012, when I noticed a thin dark streak in the sky coming up from behind the foothills. My heart beat faster as I stopped at the local coffee shop to see if anyone had any information. They didn't. I headed up the canyon past our turnoff to see where the smoke was coming from.

As I crested the top of a large hill, I could make out a thick smoke column in a westerly direction so far away I thought it must be near Rocky Mountain National Park. I snapped several pictures on my phone, turned around, and headed back down the canyon. I wound up the last two and half miles on the dirt road to our property. Joel had left earlier that morning and was already there. My words spilled out quickly as I told him what I had seen; he had seen it too. But we both thought it wouldn't amount to much, and I tried to calm myself down as I went to work painting the mudroom.

As the afternoon went by, it became very windy until I could hear it howling at top speed through the trees. The sky above our house had gone from cobalt blue to orange black in a matter of hours. The thin dark streak had exploded into a monstrous dark cloud that caused the sun to disappear. The acrid smell of smoke permeated the air and was noticeable inside the house. Joel and I went outside to take a few pictures of the apocalyptic and eerie scene.

We returned to our work inside for a few more hours. It was just before dark when I caught a glimpse of flashing red and white lights outside in the driveway. It was the canyon fire chief who said we were under a mandatory evacuation for a wildfire more than thirteen miles away.

My first thought was that they were being very cautious after a wildfire in the state had claimed several lives. After the fire chief left, Joel and I looked at each other in confusion. What do we do? Take the washer and dryer that had just been installed and put it in the truck? What about the temporary propane tanks near the house? What about our skid steer? Are there any trees that we should cut down? We reasoned that the fire probably wasn't going to travel all those miles and burn down our house. But just in case, I went into practical mode and started giving orders.

As a registered nurse, this was my natural response in stressful times. All the construction debris was piled outside away from the house. The propane tanks were hauled down the driveway. I told Joel to get all the power tools that he could fit in the truck. I went into our shed and grabbed my pink tool belt, along with Joel's brown one. Joel moved our trusty skid steer that had been bought with years of savings into the most open area of the driveway.

With both cars loaded, we walked around inside the house one last time. It was dark now, and we knew it was time to go. Joel and I stood in our living room gazing through the eastern windows at the glowing lights from town below. We wrapped our arms around each other in an embrace and we spent the last moments swaying gently to an unsung melody—our first dance in our new house. We had no idea this would be the final memory of our new house or that it would be forever engraved in our souls.

Back at our rental, that night was spent tossing and turning in bed. The next days were a blur as we watched the High Park fire burn out of control, attended twice daily briefings for residents, and updated family while ash fell out of the sky in town. Surely our house wouldn't burn, I thought. It would be such a cruel joke that it didn't even seem possible.

It was during a morning briefing on the third day that the sheriff, in a choked voice, informed the crowd that the wildfire had burned through a large area overnight and many homes had been lost. There was a collective gasp in the room that I will never forget. Up until then I had hoped our house was still standing, but now I barely held back the sobs that threatened to escape from my throat. I frantically drove from the briefing to an overview on the western side of town where Joel had been using a spotting scope to see if the house was still there.

The area was packed with people who were watching the fire, and vehicles lined the roadway in both directions. My heart was pounding when I pulled over on the shoulder of the road and caught sight of Joel on the other side. As I waited for a break in the traffic, I yelled across the road to him, "Is it still there?" When he didn't answer, I wasn't sure if he had heard me or not. Crossing the road, I yelled again, "Is it still there?"

He was looking at me but didn't speak. Annoyed, I asked him a third time when he grabbed me tight and started crying and told me our house was gone. I was in disbelief, hugging him with one arm while worrying about spilling the container of yogurt I had in my other hand.

We stood there in a half embrace on the gravel shoulder of the road while I tried to console my husband while feeling absolutely numb inside.

We sat in the grass on the side of the road for what felt like hours in shock. Grayish black smoke had shrouded the foothills and with nothing left to do, we went back to the rental. It was then that it hit me and we both alternated between saying we couldn't believe it and doubling over with deep, racking sobs. A day later a volunteer firefighter who lived near our property left a message on our answering machine confirming our house had burned completely to the ground.

Afterwards, friends and coworkers stopped by with meals and words of encouragement as we attempted the motions of daily living. We were in a daze, unable to really process what had just happened. Our families kept asking if we were really sure that a wildfire had burned down our beloved house. A detached unemotional side of me had been curious as to what would be left after a wildfire. It seemed surreal to have both types of thoughts in the same head.

I had difficulty comprehending how life was going on for those unaffected by the fire. While driving one day, I got angry when I saw a person laughing in another car. Don't they know what had happened? How can they laugh when I am broken inside? Worse yet, our rental was for sale and we had to move. Not to our dream home but to yet *another* rental. Meanwhile, the High Park fire continued to rage for almost three more weeks before it was contained and we were allowed to return to our property.

When residents in the burn area were allowed back, we drove up the charred canyon to our property. There were a few homes that had survived but most had been lost. As we turned into our driveway, it was a mess of burnt trees, downed power lines, and rocks whose surfaces had literally crumbled from the heat. Before cresting the small hill that hid the house site from view, I prayed for a miracle. But it was gone.

There was a large hole with unrecognizable shapes that turned out to be half melted appliances mixed with friable concrete chunks. The supporting steel I-beams had partially melted and collapsed into the foundation. There was no trace of the beautiful wooden beams that made up the timber frame. Sections of metal roofing were scattered all over the place in twisted reddish heaps.

The air was heavy with the smell of smoke and ash covered everything. The skid steer's aluminum parts had melted and left silver colored liquid pooled on the ground. Joel and I held each other as we gazed across miles of burnt forests and at the debris that had been our house of dreams. Shattered, we drove away in silence, passing neighbors who were also weeping at what was no more.

The unspoken question remained; what to do now? The regular meetings by the nonprofit organization United Policyholder's became a support group of sorts, all of us trying to negotiate the homeowner's insurance claims that seemed to add insult to injury. We negotiated the unfamiliar terrain of paperwork and inventories.

Meanwhile, lurking in the back of our minds was the question—do we rebuild? I didn't think I could live on the lifeless, blackened landscape of what used to be our wilderness refuge.

Everything I knew to be true had been thrown upside down and backwards. I felt like I didn't know which way was up. I questioned everything: my spirituality, the concept of fairness, and life in general. I felt all sorts of emotions that warred for my attention. I began to swear a lot more, drink a little more, and wondered why I had waited for something for so long only to have it taken away.

I lost weight, stopped exercising, and hunkered down in a state of awfulness. In the midst of the chaos, I had to return to work and finish the credits for a second bachelor's degree while trying to find my way in the still murky air.

We started looking at houses for sale as a way to figure out what we wanted to do. A large volleyball court across the street with industrial sized spotlights was the only reason we didn't buy a log home that was the first on our list to look at. After that, there wasn't anything that appealed to us. It wasn't until later that Joel and I were able to shape our minds in asking what *could be* instead of *what was* when looking at our property.

After months of grieving, questioning, and thinking, we made the decision to rebuild. A few things were certain. First, we wanted a completely different house to honor the first one where so much love, sweat, and tears had gone into its making. It was truly irreplaceable. Second, we were going to hire someone to build it for us. Joel had worked tirelessly at his office job while also building the house for all those months. He was exhausted both physically and emotionally and simply could not do it again.

In late fall of 2012, we met with our builders and started working on a new set of plans, ready to try and start again. By focusing on the design of the second house, I felt a little glimmer of hope of what was to come. I could smile through the tears as our builders gently eased us into the process again. They waited patiently for our decisions. But I still wanted to scream that it wasn't fair, that my husband had worked so hard for so long and now a piece of us was missing forever.

Well-meaning acquaintances said, "At least you didn't lose all your stuff." But little did they know that the house *was our stuff.* I would have gladly traded every personal belonging that I owned to have my house back. The tiles I had lovingly picked out for the shower wall, the fern fossil in the rock to the left of the mantle, and the stained concrete floor…that was our stuff. It was difficult to explain but having my heart on my sleeve, I tried vainly anyway. I tried to get excited for our new home but at times I dissolved into tears driving away from our builder's shop. I just wanted my house back.

Spring of 2013 came and a freshly dug foundation stood atop our old house footprint. The first house remains had been scraped from the rocky soil and hauled away. It felt good to have it gone. Soon Douglas fir timbers outlined the shape of our second house, and the sounds of nail guns and air compressors echoed the newly opened landscape. We planted little yearling ponderosa pines to make up for the hundreds of trees we had lost. I was overjoyed to nurture something living and green. We celebrated when we found a small cactus that had returned after the fire.

During the year it took to build the second house, we experienced construction setbacks, cost overruns, and delays with our mortgage company with a multitude of emotions. At times, the rebuilding was excruciating. Plain and simple, I was worn out and missed home. It was especially bitter when a failed final inspection in late March of 2014 found our two cats and us unexpectedly homeless. Thankfully, a dear friend made arrangements for us to stay temporarily at her father's house. We simply couldn't have made it through the nightmare of losing our home without the love and support of our friends and family.

We moved into our new house on April 8, 2014, with a mix of joy and deep sadness. I wanted to think that I was tough and had triumphed over the fire that had taken so much. This was symbolized by the outline of a phoenix on either side of our new chimney. But the truth was I still felt more like the ashes consumed by the flame than the rebirth following it.

The house we lost had felt like home long before it had even been completed, but this second house was going to take time; the amount of which was unknown. I felt comforted by other women who had suffered the loss of their homes to the flame. This kinship of kindred souls applied balm to the still raw areas of my heart. And like the green grasses that returned in the warm summer months, I too will heal in nature's time.

CANYON SPIRIT

BONNIE ANTICH

O ur mountain community is in the Upper Buckhorn Canyon, a small remote canyon in northern Colorado. This small community experienced three disasters in three years: two fires, and a flash flood caused by heavy rains rushing through the burn areas.

I'm no stranger to forest fire. I was a firefighter for four years while working for the U.S. Forest Service in my early thirties. In the summer of 1989, we went to Idaho for three weeks and fought fires, right alongside the Pike Hotshots from Colorado. We had an amazing crew boss who was very well known in firefighting circles. Due to his expertise, we were the first to arrive on fires. Whereas before, with less experienced crew bosses, we mostly did "mop up" which was a completely different aspect of firefighting.

Lightning storms ignited 335 fires in the Boise and Payette National Forests over the course of eight days that summer, eventually burning 46,000 acres of land. Our crew would hang out around the helicopter pad just waiting for the inevitable lightning strike to hit in the hills. When one struck, a helicopter would take two of us to the spot and drop us off for the night. The next day we would be picked up again when we had the spot fire completely out. We carried the bare minimums—our firefighting gear, our sleeping bag, and a Meal Ready to Eat (MRE). It was a highlight of my life to work with such an amazing crew boss in that summer.

Once after two solid weeks of fighting fires with no time off in between, we went to a local bar in Idaho City to unwind. I was blown away at the welcome we received by the locals—they were so happy to have us there trying to save their town and everything they cared about.

You might think that my firefighting background prepared me for the disasters that hit closer to home, but it's one thing to fight a wildland fire, and it's another thing to helplessly watch it destroy homes and take lives.

Just south and east of our property, the Crystal fire in 2011 was caused by human carelessness. Thirteen homes were lost—one of which was the home of our very dear friends. Evacuated during the fire, we had a few extremely nerve-wracking days. In order to return home, we had to pass through a guarded roadblock and show our drivers licenses to prove we lived in the area. It was a huge relief to know that our home was spared and that no lives were lost, but we worried extensively about neighbors who had lost their homes. I was consumed with finding out where our friends were so I could help them, and finally discovering that they were safely staying with friends in town.

The High Park fire in 2012 was caused by a lightning strike just a half-mile north of our property. During the evacuation, sheriff's deputies went door-to-door informing us we had to head to the top of our canyon because the fire had jumped the road at the bottom, making it impassable. Arriving at the top, we found the gate locked and nervously waited for someone to arrive with the key.

For three anxiety filled weeks, we lived in our vacant rental property in Fort Collins, and a host of friends, neighbors and their pets stayed with us. As we gathered together each day for news on the fire, we were shocked at how fast the fire was spreading and the amount of devastation it was causing.

Our homes were under continuous threat for weeks, but somehow for our little group, all of our homes managed to survive. Upon returning home, we discovered that the fire came within 100 yards of our property. The burned area was massive. Two hundred and fifty-nine homes were lost and numerous others were damaged, leaving many of our friends and neighbors homeless.

I had deep compassion for our local firefighters. They had their hands full and were on their own without much backup in the beginning when the fire took off and destroyed the homes of their friends and neighbors, along with some of their own homes. My husband Scotty and I were listening to the ham radio, and we could hear our fire department under extreme duress. The fire was raging out of control, due to the wind, and those fire fighters knew the owner of each home personally.

We knew they felt almost as helpless as we did. Whenever there is a fire, I know that those fighting it are doing the best they can and are working extremely hard. This was the first time I had experienced such a huge fire on a personal level with so many homes being lost and lives being threatened. We were all part of the same small community and all at risk. I'm pretty sure I had PTSD then, although I didn't recognize it as such.

Then the Colorado Floods occurred in 2013 and we were in the thick of disaster once again. This time, 1,500 homes were destroyed and countless more were damaged. I was out of town visiting a friend during the flash flood but my husband and three pets (which I consider to be my children) were stranded at the house. The dirt road in front of our home turned into a river as it was completely washed away by the normally gentle creek. Scotty decided that he and our dog would be able to hike out if necessary but not the cats, so he put them in their travel cages and drove them to the evacuation helicopter. He and our dog remained home for another week in order to protect our property and help neighbors who were also staying.

Scotty helped FEMA by picking up a neighbor who needed to be evacuated on the helicopter and by clearing properties to be sure all the people stranded were ok. After Scotty evacuated we were told that we would not be able to return until the following spring due to the extensive damage. During the time we were evacuated we were given permission to drive a private four-wheel drive road near our canyon. Every weekend we drove as far as we could, then hiked another hour with our dog to our property to clean up what we could and fill our backpacks with important items we needed while living in Fort Collins. Thankfully, three months after the flood we learned our road had been restored enough to be passable and that we could return home.

After we moved back home, I continued to experience anxiety, confusion, guilt, and depression. I found it hard to reach out to anyone. With the help of a friend, I finally realized I had survivor's guilt and PTSD. To this day, I still have a low tolerance for stress and am over emotional. I still tend to hide out and then feel guilty that I am avoiding others. I'm working on taking care of myself and have been going to therapy and receive Eye Movement Desensitization and Reprocessing (EMDR) therapy, which has been working well in releasing and relieving my symptoms.

I know that many of my friends, neighbors, and community as a whole are also still recovering. I've always been a very sensitive person and I feel very deeply, especially when it comes to the suffering of humans and animals. I'm not totally sure what I'm hoping for in writing this story. It's not sympathy, but perhaps it's just a chance to speak the truth of what I've been going through. I haven't been able to socialize in person or online because I get so easily overloaded. Yet, I still believe I am a very strong person, and I expect to find my spirit again. Perhaps some of the ways I have changed will be permanent. I'm still not sure. I do know that I used to be happier than I am now—and I am determined to be that happy person again.

After the fires, and while working in my flower garden, I was jolted by the thought "How dare I enjoy such pleasures while so many friends and neighbors have lost their homes?" I felt I was not entitled to feel my pain since I didn't lose my home. I wanted so badly to help everyone and to ease their suffering in some way, and I felt so frustrated and guilty because I couldn't figure out how. I kept thinking that if I just give it time I would return to a happier me. Then the floods happened and my PTSD symptoms became much more severe and that's when a friend persuaded me to do something about it. I had truly lost my spirit and I had to admit it. I started therapy and began to learn new coping strategies.

I believe I am and always will be a very caring and loving person. I share my story in hopes that in some small way it may help others who have struggled as I did in dealing with survivor's guilt. In the meantime, I continue to find the most small and precious things to celebrate and have gratitude for. There really are so very many things! I am healing and can see my progress. I will continue loving and caring for others, the animals, the planet, and myself.

I am committed to grow and will accept nothing less for myself, even if that means seeking help to do so. It may take time, and it may not always be pretty, but I will grow nonetheless. I believe that is why I am here. I will take the necessary steps to heal and I will do it with love, gratitude, and compassion in my heart. I will regain my spirit and wish the same for my community. Throughout my life, I was always busy trying to find myself. The good part of all this is that I finally did. It just took time—and many life changes.

IRREPLACEABLE THINGS

SUSAN RUANE MCCONNELL

L ong after the Waldo Canyon fire jumped a ridge and rolled down the foothills and into my Colorado Springs neighborhood in 2012, instantly incinerating my home and 145 of my immediate neighbors' homes—essentially, most of my entire community—the all-consuming grief and loss and being lost have subsided. In their stead is a quieter, slower-to-surface ache. It shows up when I reach into a drawer to retrieve an item of clothing I no longer have. Or I begin preparing a recipe in the kitchen and realize all over again I've yet to replace the stick blender essential to one of the steps. Or a tune on the radio summons the memory of The Flying W Wranglers, whose songs drifted across the nearby ranch to my front porch on summer evenings, year in and year out.

Some days, all this time later, I walk into the house where I now live, far from the foothills and swooshing breezes, and experience a surreal disorientation. I take in the different furnishings, different colors, different floor plan, different light. All these things combine, more or less, in a pleasing way and yet my reaction is unsettling, visceral. *How the hell did I get here?*

I could tell you my now not-so-unique story, reiterating what it was like to stand before a smoking pit that once was my house and see into an unending vista of charred and broken landscape, seeing where and what I shouldn't have been able to see, feeling I'd landed on some grotesque, uninhabitable planet that sucked all breath from my lungs and emptied a monsoon from my eyes.

I might speak of the following sleepless weeks, and the months and months of maniacal obsession to complete an insurance claim that would only cover fifty-four percent of my actual loss, and the panic that set in when the first snow came the next winter and I had no boots. Or shovel. Or hat. Or mittens.

Starting from scratch after a total loss is a process with a defined beginning and no discernible ending; it is a journey without map or schedule. I continue to discover that it simply takes as long as it takes… and mine's still taking.

The fire took my home from me, and every little and big thing in it. With all good intentions, people will (and did and do still) utter a variety of well-intended platitudes to cast a positive spin. *You're lucky—you'll get a whole new wardrobe. You get to buy all new furniture. At least you're alive.* But the one that surely arrives as fingernails across chalkboard: *things can be replaced.*

If only that were perfectly, unequivocally, matter-of-factly true. But it's not.

Consider the story of my little chest of drawers, and other first *things* that launched me into and carried me through my grown-up life.

I first met up with the chest in 1976, after it was pulled from the dank, cobwebby basement at one of my grandmothers' houses.

It was unremarkable, nothing special to look at—the wood was dry and cracked in places and the drawers had lost all glide— but it came from someone I loved, whose artistic soul and homemaking panache I admired. Someone who loved me, quietly but with aplomb, who wanted to contribute to my start in the adult world. I also needed what the chest had to offer. In the ensuing decades, I would transform it several times over into many kinds of special.

I was then a full-time sophomore in college with an almost full-time job to pay for the tuition as well as a lifestyle outside of a dormitory. I'd rented my first solo apartment— a one bedroom, corner unit on Dale Street in the aging St. Louis suburb of Richmond Heights.

My unit was one of eight in an unadorned, squat brick building that more resembled a prison than residence. Nonetheless, the apartment felt grand with its voluminous kitchen; its tidy, black and white tiled bath and porcelain pedestal sink; a decent-sized living room; and a small bedroom with the thinnest excuse for a closet. Hardwood floors ran throughout, and the wood entry door with frosted glass panes glanced across the hall landing to a twin.

Every room had glass to bring in light: a window above the tub; four in the living room; three in the bedroom; and one in the kitchen. The windowed back door afforded even more light and an expanded view to a slice of a metal-railed cement patio, tucked under a set of fire escape stairs.

Almost directly across the street sat an auto repair shop—and beefy, black-spectacled, hairy-forearmed Wayne, who would come to crush on me and fix my metallic green '64 Volkswagen Beetle on the cheap when it not infrequently acted up.

All things considered, my nineteen-year-old self felt like she'd hit the jackpot.

In that beguiling, freshly white-walled apartment came the heady rush of independence and first tries at defining home on my terms and with my own unique style. My first furnishings were paltry: a small, nondescript dresser and a rough-grained oak telephone table, leftovers after a great grandmother was moved to a nursing home; a full-sized mattress and box spring set, plunked on the floor; and a handmade occasional table with inlaid wood top. It was a special treasure, not merely for its good looks but because it was the first piece of furniture I ever purchased, rescued from a musty, crowded Salvation Army thrift store down on a sketchy stretch of Forest Park Boulevard. I flanked the table with two canary-yellow, canvas-over-metal butterfly chairs… pilfered from my other grandmother's back yard.

I brought more into the apartment: a laminate-top kitchen table with four vinyl and chrome chairs; a rust and gold plaid polyester hide-a-bed sofa; a chunky Craftsmen-style coat tree; a simple, short and long bookcase that would eventually double up as plant stand and television perch. I bought second-hand filing cabinets, got an old flat-planed door, and set up a desk.

The kitchen, though, was poorly appointed. It offered an ancient gas stove, old farmhouse-style sink with ribbed drain board, open to the floor below, and a noisy refrigerator so petite that even I, at 5'2", could see its top. There was just one cabinet, above the sink, and it wasn't enough.

In came the unassuming little four-drawer chest. It fit perfectly with its back against the stove's side, and it adequately stored silverware and small gadgets and dishcloths. While functional, it was also as plain vanilla and uninspiring as the long expanse of white wall on the other side of the room.

When I got permission from the landlord to paint, he probably wasn't imagining the loud fuchsia, gold and purple stripes I'd sashay diagonally up that wall and down another. Not long after the walls got dressed, Grandma's little chest got its first coat of paint, too—a vivid tangerine orange.

I didn't foresee it, but that bright and happy chest would be the first in a lifetime of creative, one-of-a-kind furniture painting.

Eventually, of course, I moved on from Dale Street—to another apartment, another state, condos, town homes, and other houses. My early possessions trickled along with me, and then not, as life grew and needs changed and style matured.

But the little chest soldiered along with me, through marriage and children and divorce and nest emptying. It changed drawer pulls and wore new coats of different colors; it was stripped down and stained; stripped again and painted. It sat in hallways, next to chairs, and alongside a few beds, holding toys and tools, linens and orphaned leftovers. It was the only material piece connecting me to that grandmother, those first days of independence, and all the ensuing days of my curlicued adult life.

When my grandmother died, peacefully but frustrated—she was ninety-nine and so hoping to see one hundred—I was compelled yet again to bring new life to the little chest.

I layered on several coats of glossy black, found a stencil I liked and dabbed through it with a happy, grass-green acrylic. White porcelain knobs formed the eyes of flowers. The freshly whimsical chest went next to my bed, on the side where I slept, and into it went my less worn but more precious jewelry: heirlooms such as wedding rings, antique hat pins and rhinestone hair clips; my freshman cheerleader megaphone pendant; faded obituaries; a made-from-the-other-grandma's-button-box necklace; and other small touchstones chronicling my fifty-five years of life.

I enjoyed this last incarnation of the chest only for a short while, until the fire came and annihilated it and other accumulated treasures: a vast collection of artwork; my great grandfather's rocking chair that soothed my children—and me—during their early years; the checkerboard set my son made me in ceramics class; the one-hundred-button necklace my daughter strung together in celebration of her first one hundred days of kindergarten. The 1980s rustic pine table, sprinkled with gashes and alpha-numeric indentations left over from homework assignments completed with concentrated effort. I mourn their loss. Still.

I also mourn my mother's wedding dress, which I'll never share with my daughter or anyone else, and the antique laces and linens passed on to me from multiple generations. I yearn to see and hold once more the cloisonné and blown glass frogs my late sister added to my decades-long collection.

I miss my books. Oh, so much, my books. Especially the dog-eared, spine-broken, penciled-in-the-margins ones I'd kept since high school and college. Classic literature, contemporary fiction, creative nonfiction, poetry, collections of Indian and Holocaust and Third World history and literature, and three shelves of writing reference material. As well, all my years and pages of pre-digital writings, longhand and by typewriter, that told the stories of dreams and life.

I long for the way that chest and those so many other things threaded together a life's history: moments in time, a multitude of conversations, countless celebrations, even the simple inhalations and exhalations that marked the passage from one day to the next. I want to go back and breathe in the magical air about them, that intangible, indefinable sense of home they collectively imbued.

And that's the painful rub when someone reminds me that "things can be replaced." A house can be replaced; the home that's created inside of it occurs over a lifetime.

That hasn't stopped me from trying again. It may be plain dumb luck that my insurance coverage sucked because the compensation hasn't accommodated the purchase of "all new" anything. Instead I've cultivated some dandy second-hand chops all over again and in so doing, made a heartwarming discovery— I've brought story into this house.

I don't necessarily *know* the story behind the antique chest that serves as base for the TV or whose private lives lived inside the $100 dresser or how many meals were passed at that gorgeous hunk of new-to-me dining room table. But their long lives surely hold stories and some days, many more days now, it's almost as if they are whispering and high-fiving each other over their success in making "from scratch" start to feel like home.

A home that is emerging, if you can believe it, on another Dale Street.

These days when more well-intended people find their own silver linings for me in the strange, otherworldly aftermath of total loss, I listen and sometimes even agree with them. Yes, without a doubt, I am blessed simply to be alive. I'm still not certain that I'm blessed to recreate from scratch a wardrobe, a household, a life. But I do understand that things are just things and some, indeed many, can be replaced.

But the little chest and all the other lifetime vessels of memory, emotion, progress, witness? Never.

TEMPERED, FORGED, TENSILED FREE

ASTRID

The trees are stumped and so am I
Beyond before…my eyes just dry
Months like years—days like weeks
thunder strikes charcoal creeks

I've come and gone and gone and come
To remnants of my dear lost home
Wept and gnashed my teeth at fate
Run from random thoughts to hate

…is there…something…over there?
A twinkling gleam, I forage—stare…

NOPE! Ash; all gray
stop
feel
wait…
I've found ME THERE; why hell: I RATE!

Bam! Ow! And How! Awake I git
Scared black n blue; my heart's relit
…embers grow new fire in ME.
but, next right action's just: TO BE.

I'm not—the bed, the house, the tree
I'm tempered, forged, tensiled: FREE
Thank God for life; amends I can!
pick up pieces; "know *who* I am."

FIRE ON THE MOUNTAIN

CHERYL DELANY

I *smell smoke.* There are few words that put real fear in mountain folk, but those three little words top our list. I live at just over eight thousand feet in elevation. There are no guardrails on our roads, and the air is thin, the temperatures cool. It's very secluded. "I couldn't stand to live so far away from everything. Why do you like living in the mountains?" I've been asked questions like these on numerous occasions. *Like?* Nope. I do not like it. I LOVE it. I love that I can hike for hours in my backyard. I love that I can find a herd of elk, cows, horses, deer, or the occasional bear in my front yard.

I love the swarms of hummingbirds that arrive every April like clockwork and zip around my property. I love that I know most of my neighbors. I love that we have barbecues in the summer and have each other over for dinner parties. We help each other when we get stuck in the snow, accidentally locked out of our homes, or need to borrow an egg. We depend on each other, you kind of have to when you are miles away from grocery and hardware stores. I love it in the mountains, but bad things can happen.

I will never forget one of those bad things. It was the day that a forest fire swept through our idyllic surroundings. My husband and I had been working on the property when we smelled the smoke. We, like everyone in the neighborhood, knew there had been a controlled burn a few days before, but the wind that day was insane. As my husband Isaac hopped onto his ATV and drove up the road to assess things, I started calling neighbors. The few people I reached had been told the same thing. "It's the controlled burn. Nothing to worry about."

Isaac came back with his report. To him it looked like the wind had kicked the flames of the burn back up. He assumed there were crews there to monitor it, but a few minutes later when the smoke cloud began billowing up from behind the hill in front of our house, we didn't think of calling 911, assuming again that there were crews down there monitoring the burn.

After returning from another look, my husband said we needed to be ready to leave. We hurried to load up our truck with belongings, things that we classified as important like our wedding album and family heirlooms. It's a weird thing trying to figure out what to take and what to leave. "It's just stuff," Isaac said while giving me a shrug. "All of this can be replaced."

He was right. It was all just stuff, but it was *our* stuff, and both of us had worked hard to get it. The house, we'd built *that* ourselves. A Texas girl, I had always dreamed of Colorado and living in the mountains. I loved our home and everything in it. But standing and taking all of it in, none of it was important. None of it mattered. It seemed *temporary*.

Anything can be taken from you in a flash, even your life. We both knew the truth of that. In August of 2000, the two of us had almost been killed when a nineteen-year-old girl ran a red light and hit us as we drove through an intersection on our motorcycle. Both of us looked at things differently after that. We vowed to enjoy every day we shared together no matter what. As long as we were together, we could get through it all, the good and the bad.

I took one last look at the house, wondering if it would still be there when we returned. A part of me had accepted that it wouldn't be. The wind had whipped the smoke up even more, and it looked like the world was ending. Nothing I had seen, not in a movie or on television, looked or sounded remotely like it. The wind and smoke combined to generate an evil howling. It was as if Hell had opened up a hole on earth.

As we left, we saw an emergency vehicle coming down our road to make sure everyone had been evacuated, and the serious nature of what was happening finally sank in.

Looking back, I know that we were more than fortunate. After being kept from our home for two weeks, we were able to return. Our house still stood. Except for the smell of smoke and a few charred trees, the hillside was still plush with pines. The birds still sang. I look around at everything still so beautiful on my side of the hill and I am thankful and grateful. Some of our neighbors lost everything. Some lost their lives.

The worst thing, the thing that sticks with me the most, is that I was *there* while it was happening. I was there and had no idea how bad things were on the other side of the hill. I felt like I should've done more. I think about my wonderful neighbors who are no longer with us—Samuel and Linda and Ann—and I'm angry that it didn't occur to me to go over to that part of the neighborhood to make sure everyone was safe. Most of all I'm angry at the senseless nature of it all because *it didn't have to happen.*

As human beings, it's in our nature to try to make sense out of tragedy. But as hard as we mull over it, it never will make any sense. Instead we do other things and attempt to move on. For the people in our neighborhood that means making sure nothing like the Lower North Fork fire ever happens again. We try to give our lost neighbors a voice.

By talking to news outlets, we brought attention to the negligence that caused the fire. The 911-call system which failed us has been revamped. The governor of Colorado formed a committee to investigate, although they never specifically investigated the cause of the Lower North Fork wildfire. Informative websites were placed on the Internet to get our stories out. Those who lost their homes spoke at the state capitol. Bills and legislation were passed.

The State, after some major foot-dragging, eventually compensated the people who lost everything. It was a long, tedious, and painful process, but we exposed the mistakes that were made and attempted to hold those state entities accountable. We still fight, trying to affect change in how controlled burns are regulated. I can't say that we've been successful, but the trying helps.

The memories of what happened that day still haunt us, but some of the mountain folks have rebuilt. With all the burnt trees dotting the landscape, my husband began a new business venture and Colorado Custom Sawmill was born. Sometimes we mill trees from the fire. The grain, due to the extreme temperatures the pines suffered, is rich in color with greens, reds, and chocolate browns. It's sobering to think that something as destructive as a fire could also create something so beautiful.

We've built things with wood from the fire and these pieces are displayed prominently in newly restored homes. A writing desk, doors, and window seats, they are original and beautiful works of craftsmanship and they serve as reminders. It's a sort of *screw you* gesture, as if to say, *you aren't going to run us out. We are here to stay.*

Tragedy can pull people apart, but for those of us who remain, the wildfire has brought us closer. I know more of my neighbors, the ones from over the hill, the ones I once knew only in passing. For a while I had a hard time going over to the part of the neighborhood that underwent so much damage, but I sucked it up and ventured out. Sometimes I sit where Lamb's School, the little Red School House, used to be. It was a landmark that all of us loved. The fire took that from us too, but there is talk of rebuilding or placing a memorial there.

I don't know if that's the so-called mountain spirit or just the gritty fight that all of us have inside. Maybe it's always been there. Maybe it takes some sort of bad thing, some adversity, for it to rear its head and push back; I don't really know. What I can tell you is that the view up here is still breathtaking, and when I see Pike's Peak lit up by the sunset, I think of my lost neighbors and how often they must've drunk in and appreciated the beauty of that same view. And in that moment, they are not forgotten.

THE WILDFIRE
OF BIRTH

AMANDA DEANGELIS

On June 9, 2012, my husband and I were busily working on our house up in Rist Canyon. I had plans to pick up my son in Denver that afternoon, after a visit with his grandparents. Then, I would return to Fort Collins to teach my Intuitive Childbirth Class. As I headed down the canyon, several Rist Canyon Volunteer Fire Department trucks were hurriedly making their way up the hill. Despite the fact that no words were exchanged, I caught the panic in each of the drivers' eyes. Unsure of whether there was a fire—how big or where it might be located—I called to let my husband know what I witnessed, just in case.

With my eyes fixated on the rear view mirror, I hoped that the sky above the foothills would be blue once I emerged from the canyon. My heart quickly sank as I saw a huge smoke cloud rising slowly over the mountains. Despite the visual confirmation and an uneasy feeling in the pit of my stomach, I told myself that the cloud was too far south to be of concern to us. I went about my day in denial.

At 4 o'clock that afternoon, we received a reverse 911 call. The female voice recording telling us to evacuate felt like a bucket of ice water being thrown over my head. I sobered up from my intoxicating denial and began to make mental notes about my family members. My son Nico was down in town. My husband Lou and our dog William were still up on the mountain. I would not see the two of them until 11:00 o'clock that night.

Despite the evacuation call and a visit from the sheriff, my husband refused to leave. He, along with our best friend, would spend ten hours chopping down trees at the same dizzying speed the Once-ler chopped down Truffula trees in Dr. Seuss' s *The Lorax*. With the fire quickly approaching our property, my husband found his keys, loaded the dog, and scanned the rooms trying to decide what to take. The only thing he grabbed were my wedding rings, passed down from his mother.

The next three days were hard for our family. Staying at a friend's house, we laid awake each night listening to the winds whip ferociously. We thought about all that could be lost and how we would rebuild our lives. No insurance, no house, no personal belongings. It was daunting to imagine a life without *anything,* but I would be lying if I told you we didn't think about this a lot in those seventy-two hours.

The stress of the uncertainty and the barrage of insensitive questions regarding our failure to get insurance, or grab our belongings, could very well have left me in despair. I chose instead to remain in the eye of the storm. It calmed me to believe that regardless of the outcome, we would get through it. I remained unapologetic for the choices we had made. I also had a tremendous amount of faith in my husband and his efforts to preserve our lives. These thoughts, along with the outpouring of community support, helped me to stay at peace while we awaited word on our structures.

On June 12, we found out that our house and our whole life had survived. It was three weeks before we were allowed to return, and when we did make our journey up the canyon, it was with both joy and sadness. The only way I knew how to make sense of my new surroundings was to totally immerse myself in them. Each day I would take long hikes and bring my camera. Everywhere I looked was a photo opportunity.

The forest was magnificently metallic and naked. Tree trunks were twisted, turned, and looped around themselves. Green grass was sprouting up everywhere. Woodpeckers were busily making homes in the still standing snags. This charred forest was not dead. It was not destroyed. And it was not a disaster. This was just life. The beginning of a new cycle had begun and it was nothing to fear.

The media was abuzz, describing the fire as a *gruesome battle, combat, a fight, and a natural disaster*. We were *victims*. Governor Hickenlooper said *nature is conspiring against us*. I started paying special attention to the jargon being used during this time and it got me thinking about a similar topic that I talk about in the birthing class I teach—language.

We discuss the importance of words and language when considering how a caregiver speaks to a mother during their journey through pregnancy and birth. Does a caregiver *ask* or *tell* things. For instance, would a caregiver *ask you* if *you wanted to try* having a natural birth or would your caregiver *tell you that they would let you try* for a natural birth? A small difference in words can make a huge difference in the way the situation and the outcome are experienced.

Between the photographs I took, my years of experience as a doula and a childbirth educator, and my attention to the language used during this wildfire, a theory sparked. Wildfire is no different than natural birth. Both are thought to be destructive or painful with no real lasting benefit. Both are considered an "evil" that needs to be suppressed or dulled, and they are both treated with disrespect and feared by the general public.

I pondered: are wildfires truly destructive, and is birth truly painful with no real lasting benefit? Fire is an elemental and critical force in nature and it is imperative for the forest's renewal. Birth is a normal and natural physiological process that helps a mother discover her very deepest self, thus preparing her for the difficult job of mothering.

In fire-adapted ecosystems, many species and plants have evolved ways of avoiding or surviving fires and even some, still, are dependent on fire for habitat or nutrients. The pain experienced in childbirth is met with an ingenious system of endorphin levels that rise correspondingly. As a mother experiences more pain, her body creates natural opiates to help her through labor.

The lodgepole pine has what is called a serotinous cone that is filled with seeds and held together by resin. This cone can only be opened by very high temperatures, which melt the resin. These seeds are then released into the ground during a wildfire and are responsible for the start of new lodgepole pines.

Pain in labor is a special type of pain. It is one that almost always does not cause any damage to the body. After a woman has worked her way through childbirth, she learns more about her own capabilities and that of her child. This knowledge can give birth to a whole new confidence in life.

Is it necessary to suppress wildfires and to dull or mask the pain of childbirth? Quite the contrary really.

We now know in fire-adapted forests, fire suppression rather than fire itself causes more disharmony and detriment to that area. The ecosystem becomes stagnant and unhealthy. Fire suppression is also very costly.

When pain medication is used (which is 90 percent of the time), it can prolong labor, it may require the need for intervention, and it affects bonding between mother and baby. It is also costly.

Why, then, is the natural cycle of both wildfire and birth treated disrespectfully and feared by the general public? Lack of education. Unfortunately, much of the wisdom regarding basic life cycles has not been passed on. Whether it is the migration of societies into cities or the growing use of technology and medicine in childbirth, our children and young adults rarely have experiences with the natural world and its processes.

In Tom Wolf's book *In Fire's Way*, he states, "It seems that the less familiar children are with real forests, the more likely they are as adults to want the government to suppress all fires." Change a couple of words around in that sentence and you have "The less familiar children are with natural birth, the more likely they are as adults to want hospitals to suppress all pain."

While we as humans often take credit for containing or suppressing a fire, it is most often a change of the elements that makes this happen. Similarly, when a woman enters the hospital during labor, often times her body will intuitively slow things up based on the new surroundings. The miraculous female system ebb and flows with the environment.

No matter how much we think we know about ecosystems or the act of giving birth, there are still aspects that elude us, and this gives rise to the anxiety we feel about them. Our greatest fear with both wildfires and natural birth is that in our attempt to control them as humans and with our technology, we know we cannot. To think that there is something outside of our control puts us in the hands of the universe, not in the driver's seat.

Today it is commonplace to blame wildfires for their destruction of homes or to blame women for their "failure to progress" during labor. In actuality it is our inability to live with nature and our lack of faith in women that is responsible for the destruction of our natural, ingenious, and healthy life cycles.

I will be honest when I tell you that there have been many times that I have cursed the fire for taking away all my shade trees, for destroying my neighbors' homes, and for the floods that have ensued. I have cursed the abuse I witness in our maternity care system too. But then I revisit the calmness in my heart that I had during the High Park fire and trust in the wisdom of Mother Nature.

These charred forests have taught me so much more than just how to readjust to a new landscape. They have taught me that in all aspects of life, there will be pain, death, and renewal. These aspects that we so often associate with fear are not to be feared. They are responsible for our growth, our health, and help us to be the people we know we can be, living in peace with the natural world.

The Thoughtful
Side of Insanity

AnnMarie Arbo

The most painful story I have to tell about the High Park fire is when a little boy asked me if his house hurt when it burned up. What do you tell a child who did not see his house burn because he, along with his family, pets, and other bits and pieces evacuated before houses began exploding? He was at the evacuation center, where he watched many of the houses in Colorado Springs go up in flames prompting the question "Did my house hurt when it burnt up?" His mother looked horrified and left it to me to answer—and I spoke, as I would have to any of my children as a mum.

"What do you think?" I said. Pondering this for a moment, he said, "I think it might have." Then after being quiet for a while, tears forming in his eyes, he asked "what about my teddy? Do you think the fire hurt him?" I thought carefully how to respond and felt I needed to be honest, so I said, "Yes, but I don't think it hurt that much as it was probably very quick." He said, "OK." Then we talked a little more and I asked if he could use another teddy, so we went and found a new one.

Children are easier to help than adults, as their pain is immediate. With grown-ups, the hurt is much deeper and harder to overcome. As a case manager, my own hurt comes from not being able to do anything until the family is ready or money is available to help them. I feel the pain of their debt and can sense the general breaking point of the family. If I think of each case as a family, rather than individuals, I can think things through better, and it is easier to help. This is how I operated for nine years as the executive director running a homeless shelter for families.

There have been times when I felt like a steamroller had plowed over me. I was road-kill on the pavement, no arms or legs, just a long flat piece of tar. Helpless, I listened to stories, knowing there was nothing I could do. Hearing family's problems I could not change, like having no home for the holidays or no insurance, was heart wrenching. Often I watched a husband and wife fighting like a couple of World War II enemies and I wanted to bang their silly heads together.

There are stories that made me want to open my purse, take out the check book, and empty my account, then turn around and have a yard sale each week for the next goodness knows how many months to get everything the family needs so there would be no more debts to bear. There are families that come in and have it all together, and I really don't need to help them; they talk lovingly to each other, and they plan in the order of what needs to be done. When I ask if there is anything they need me for they look at me and say, "Yes, you have to walk through this with us. We cannot do it on our own." Oh, the joys of human resilience; the heart and soul of a human being and the desire to survive are strong.

Then there's the hidden world of "the Forms" that need to be completed. Oh my goodness, that's hard. The family is distraught and I have to bring out this great big pile of paperwork and then have the nerve to ask for more from them, copies of this and copies of that. Forms, forms and more forms—some of them I don't even know why they are asked for. Nothing comes easy, even when there is a huge disaster.

Sometimes I feel like a fool who can do nothing to help. But I know I *can* listen and through listening I begin to make sense out of all the insanity. Some of the biggest insanity comes from insurance coverage or (sadly) lack there of. I remember one lady telling me she was underinsured because life was so busy that she never got around to upping the insurance policy, even though fires had happened in Colorado the summer before.

Can you blame someone for lack of insurance, because life does happen and other things do take preference? It was fun sometimes to be able to ask the insurance company how much they charge for a bit of compassion, no… I didn't really ask but it would have been so easy to ask that question. I do hope when all of the fires and floods are over there can be some changes made to the way insurance requests are handled!

When I gained confidence from a family, it made going forward much easier. It amazes me the way a family will let this old Brit take over and guide them through hurdles and sideswipes, common to everyone. It is easier for me to talk with suppliers, companies, and other entities that I felt could stand giving away a little bit to help families. Asking for help is not something that comes easily to survivors of any kind of disaster, but it is amazing that the people hurt the most are the ones that give the most. How does this trust develop, because they did not know me and I did not know them before all of this happened.

Everything went along well for a while, after the fire. Then the first good amount of rain came and some of the roads just washed away, trees felled for log cabins rolled down the hill. Then came the major flood of September 2013 and all of the sorrow happened again; the logs didn't just roll down the mountain a ways, they disappeared and were gone forever. FEMA became involved, as the flooding lower down was astonishing, far worse than the 1976 flood. My families, who lost homes in the fire, faced loss again in the newest disaster. So the hardest part of my case management—trust—started all over again.

What have I learned from all of you fire survivors? First, your trust in me is very special and it helps me make sense of the strength people have. You are all funny, even when you don't realize you are. While telling me your stories, you make them have humor somewhere so it is not all sad, but when I get a little deeper with you, none of it is funny. Your ability to think about others when all you needed to do was think about your own family was remarkable.

Human nature comes through when it is allowed to. Instead of worrying about your own land, you cared about the person living below you, worrying their home would be damaged from rains because the fire left nothing to absorb the rain. I saw your generosity at Christmas time—a little further on than others, you wanted to do something for a family who suffered, so you gave gifts.

Thank you for allowing me to help and become part of your families. I have many invitations to come drink a cup of tea or sip a glass of wine on all the decks, or in the yards and houses that have risen again from the flames. The memories, stories, and friendships will last just as the clouds keep rolling on over these majestic mountains. Most of all, I thank you for the care you have all shown to each other. My admiration for you is huge, but my love for you is even greater.

FOR BETTER
OR FOR WORSE

LINDA MASTERSON

It had taken us forever to find the perfect spot in the mountains to build the home we'd always dreamed about. And two more years to turn those daydreams into a sturdy log home perched on top of a ridge in the Buckhorn Canyon with views stretching out all directions. It was forty-five minutes to the nearest stoplight, and several lifetimes away from the high-pressure jobs we left behind.

It was April of 2000 when we moved in; eleven years later to the day the Crystal fire burned our dreams to the ground. By the next morning, a smoldering pile of rubble was all that remained. After a lifetime of hard work, everything we owned fit in the back of our car. All we had left was each other.

Losing your home and everything you own is a profoundly life-altering experience. It earns you a lifetime membership in a small and exclusive club no one wants to belong to. You don't get over it. You gradually come to accept that the loss will always be part of you and start moving forward, trusting that something else will someday fill the void and push it into the shadows of "remember when?"

When people ask you what you need, you laugh and shake your head. Where do you start? The only honest answer is "everything." We had to buy notebooks and pens so we could work on our claim and old clothes and boots so we could sift through our debris. I will forever be grateful to the woman at the Loveland Goodwill who unearthed a cozy robe they'd put away when they filled the racks with summer clothes.

Even today, every time some well-meaning person says "Thank God you got out alive; everything else is just stuff that can be replaced," I cringe. Your refrigerator and TV are stuff. The charm bracelet you'd had since you were a girl, the rocking horse your dad made when you were a baby, the quilts stitched by your great-grandmother…those things are not stuff. They're the fabric of your life.

There are days you think you can't go on. But you do. Because otherwise the fire will destroy your future as well as your past. Bit by bit and piece by piece you find your way back. For a long time it's like working an all-black puzzle with no corner pieces. But eventually you find one that fits, and a new picture starts to emerge.

I remember picking my way around still smoldering stump holes with our adjustor, taking photos and staring in shell-shocked wonder at the utter and complete devastation.

I remember standing by a blackened, twisted skeleton of a two-hundred-year-old ponderosa pine and saying, "So, since the house is a total loss, will they just write us a check for our policy maximum?"

And I remember him looking at me and shaking his head. "I wish we could, but it just doesn't work that way."

That was my first clue as to how little we really knew about how our insurance worked.

Insurance horror stories abound, but ours was more of a grueling marathon. Luckily we had good insurance; but like so many people, we just didn't have enough of it. Our adjustor told us that his job was to help us collect every cent we had coming. Our heads swam as he walked us through all the various coverage provisions and what we'd need to do to collect on each of them.

We learned that the first step down that long and bumpy road to recovery was listing and valuing every single thing we'd lost, from the spices in the kitchen cupboard to the albums full of family photos. We needed to show when we'd acquired it, how much it cost, and what it would cost to replace it today. Our final contents inventory listed twenty-five hundred items; it would have been even longer if we hadn't been underinsured.

Many people can't face doing their inventory; it's too painful to even contemplate. We made ourselves focus on the objective—collecting our policy maximum—and treat it like a gigantic and unpleasant project dumped on us by a demanding client. We had plenty of experience eating the elephant one bite at a time; we picked up our knives and forks and dug in.

We couldn't sleep much those first few months; every time I closed my eyes I saw the fire devouring something else I loved. There were days I got up at four in the morning and didn't stop typing until after the sun went down. Gradually, we whittled the elephant down to the size of a hippo.

Our life unrolled in reverse as I cataloged everything we used to own, trying not to think about it too much, trying to focus only on what it's worth and not think about what it meant to us. How do you value things like that box of old family snapshots (figure the cost of film and developing) or your husband's bronzed baby shoes (consult collectible websites and auction results) or the rocking horse your dad made for you when you were a baby (look up vintage handcrafted toys.)

I learned that my ancient button-fly Levis and classic LPs were worth ten times as much as my three-year-old jeans and almost-new CDs because antiques and collectibles actually appreciate in value instead of depreciate. And I learned that a notebook crammed with family recipes is worth the price of a notebook.

After it's all over, our inventory log became a memory book of sorts—the only real record we had of what our life used to be. Those well-thumbed pages are reminders of a past that now exists only on paper and in memories that are slowly fraying around the edges.

Then we did the same thing all over again for our "structure," aka our home. We were astonished to find out that our ten-year-old log house would cost twice as much to rebuild as it cost to build in the first place. We didn't have twice as much insurance, but that was our own fault.

The task of starting over is overwhelming. If you had a crazy-busy life before, it's twice as busy now. And three times as hard, because you only have about half a brain. It helps to see the glass half full, and to be grateful for what you had while you mourn what you lost. You learn that you are stronger than you thought, and that if you can laugh at yourself, you can get through anything.

Many people wrestle long and hard with what comes next. Whether to be brave pioneers and defiantly rebuild, patiently waiting for Mother Nature to make them whole, or find another place not yet ravaged and try to dream again, or slink off, defeated, to dreaded civilization, being forced to admit to yourselves and the rest of the world that you are not made of the same stuff as real wildland people.

We didn't want to do any of those things. We had loved our home and our land and our mountain community with all our heart. But everything green and beautiful that had once surrounded us was now in ashes. We couldn't really afford to buy more land and start again from scratch. We couldn't even imagine moving to town and living cheek to jowl with neighbors. Where could we put down new roots and start to grow again?

One day we walked into an old log home on a bit over three acres that had just gone on the market, and fell in love all over again. It had a beautiful view of the mountains we loved. The backyard was small by our old standards, but there were quaking aspens and a pond with a gurgling stream and goldfish with no bears and bobcats to eat them. (It turned out there were herons, though, but that's another story.) The neighbors were close enough to walk to, and far enough away for privacy.

We turned the key in the door of our new life on my birthday in late August, just about five months after the fire. It took a few more years before it started to feel like home. We shop at antique malls and thrift stores and estate sales—we don't want it to look or feel as if we ordered our new life from a catalog. Now every time we find something we love, we feel as if we're getting another piece of our life back.

We discovered that there were many things we used to own that we just didn't want or need anymore. But I also found that buying a teapot just like the one Grandma gave me helped fill in my blanks and create a link back to all those memories I was afraid would fade away.

We've always been the ones on the giving end of a helping hand. To be so badly in need for so very long was a humbling and sobering experience. Just to know that so many people were there for us was one of the greatest gifts we've ever received. We vowed that someday we would find a way to give back.

Walking through the fire changes you forever. You'll never again be able to say "What's the worst thing that can happen?" with any conviction. But it's up to you whether it changes you for better or for worse.

We had been better prepared than most, but we were nowhere near as well prepared as we could or should have been. I learned so much traveling down that long road to recovery. I didn't want anyone else to have to learn their lessons the hard way.

That's why I agreed to research and write a practical handbook for people living with wildfire risk. The last thing I wanted to do was to relive it all again on paper and research all the things we could have done better. But after a lifetime of sorting through facts for a living, I knew I was uniquely equipped to do it. I felt I had to try.

Today, *Surviving Wildfire. Get Prepared. Stay Alive. Rebuild Your Life* is being used by insurance companies and fire departments and community associations who say it gets through to people in ways they just cannot. I speak all over the country, telling people that they might not be able to control wildfire, but they are in complete control of how well prepared they are to survive, and to recover if they have to. Or as one man told me after a workshop, "Well, that was a real kick in the ass. Guess I'd better get home and do all those things I've been making excuses about."

Shortly after the fire we went up with our good friends Rex and LaVonne Ewing to see if anything could be salvaged from the remains, or if it was time to say a final good-bye and let the demolition company haul away the last of our bits and pieces.

Masked and gloved and jacketed despite the heat, we doggedly poked about in the rubble. I've always shopped year round for gifts and stored my treasures in a cupboard in the corner of the basement. LaVonne was over there industriously digging through the debris when she uncovered a big green pottery vase. Some of the glaze had melted off, but otherwise it was just fine. And here's the strangest thing of all— I'd bought that vase as a gift for her.

Of course, she wouldn't take it. So now it has a place of honor on our new mantel. It survived, just like we did. And it will go on, a bit rough around the edges, just as we will. I look at it every day, and I am reminded that we too are survivors.

FINDING MEANING
IN THE FIRE

BETHANY TRANTHAM

When I was a child, I watched the news with my parents. I remember watching Hurricane Katrina rip through New Orleans. I remember seeing images of the Hayman fire flash across my TV screen. As I watched these stories unfold before my eyes, I always had that feeling of wonder and pity for the families. I was naive and couldn't comprehend the wreckage. I was ignorant of the extent of the pain that disasters like these caused.

On March 26th of 2012, I was fourteen when we watched the news that day. "Fire," they said. This was a word I had heard countless times before. But this time was different. There was no wonder or pity. Only fear and an intense pain I wouldn't wish on my worst enemy. The breaking news update was about me. It was my life instead of a stranger's on television. It was no longer just a story. I saw it, felt it, smelled it. It affected me each moment, in every aspect of my being. How could this happen? Why me? These things happen to other people—not to me. Why?

My family lost our home to the Lower North Fork fire. It was shabby old log cabin, but it was my home. The carpets were a disgusting brown, orange, and yellow, but I grew to love that repulsive color. We had no heating system, and it was often cold, even in the summer. But we had a fireplace, along with plenty of blankets and sweatshirts to keep us warm. The water heating system was nonexistent, and the bathtub had a constant layer of grime. But I didn't mind the ripe smell of a week without a shower.

Since 1976, my family had brought family heirlooms, pictures, and other meaningful keepsakes up to the cabin. My mother's wedding dress, my great grandmother's figurines, my grandmother's handmade quilts, a hundred years in pictures of me and my family. Everything that meant anything to me was up there. My cabin was my sanctuary. It's where my heart was. To lose something that meant so much to me was devastating, like a part of my body being amputated. A piece of me was gone, and I would never get it back.

I was only fourteen. I was supposed to have the world at my fingertips. Instead, my world was shattered. I was supposed to be enjoying the spring break of my freshman year of high school, not grieving the loss of my cabin. I was supposed to be figuring out who I was and who I wanted to be. Instead, I was trying to remember how to breathe.

The next couple of years seem like a blur to me. Most of my memories have been repressed because of the pain they caused, or forgotten because they seemed so small compared to all the rest. One thing I do remember was my anger and jealousy. I looked around me and all I saw were happy people who had everything I didn't have. These dark feelings completely controlled my life. They kept me from consoling my family or neighbors who had also lost their homes. They kept me from living an honorable lifestyle.

About a year after our own fire, my father and I volunteered with the Samaritan's Purse ministry after the Black Forest fire. This was an experience that, although very healing, I am not proud of. My dad and I were helping a family sift through the remains of their once beautiful house. As can be expected, I was very emotional as this was a task that was all too fresh and raw for me.

I came to the spot where a massive oak china hutch housing dozens of collectible porcelain figurines used to stand. There was nothing left of the hutch itself, save its glass doors which were now melted together and welded to the cement floor. The figurines were scattered around the area. Most of them were broken after the wall had collapsed on top of them.

Occasionally, I would come across a figurine that was completely whole. I found myself getting jealous of the family for this. I thought, "Why do they get to keep this figurine when I have nothing?" I was literally standing in the devastating remains of this family's home, jealous of the fact that they had a couple of salvageable figurines when I didn't.

Throughout the day, we had the opportunity to talk to the family. The daughter of the victim was an emotional wreck, but her children were laughing and smiling. They appeared to be unmoved, unaffected at all by the wreckage. As the day progressed, I got angrier and angrier at these kids. They were grieving incorrectly. They were heartless and cold and insensitive, I thought.

At the end of the day, however, the volunteers presented the family with a Bible signed with notes of encouragement and hope. I cannot explain the sudden change in my heart at that moment. They looked at me with such sorrowful eyes, simply grateful for our service toward them. They weren't holding onto the loss. Instead, they were recognizing the love around them and the things they had that were still worth holding on to.

That horrible, awful, pitiful day marks the beginning of my healing process. I started to live a life thankful for the things I had, not the things I lost. It was not a perfect journey. Nor was it easy. Putting your life back together is exhausting and fragile. Even to this day, I will see or hear or even just imagine something and I will go back to a state of brokenness.

I used to have a toy farm at the cabin. It was a vintage Fisher Price "Little People Play Family Farm" manufactured in 1968. When you opened the barn door, a sound resembling a "moo" would come out. It was missing most of the pieces, but I made the most of what I had and imagined the rest. Although it is only worth about $30 on the Internet, its emotional value to me was priceless.

One day, about two years after the fire, I was watching my friend Ann's children. As I was putting her daughters to bed, my eye was drawn to something on the nightstand—a little plastic horse that I knew, without a doubt in my mind, belonged to the same set. I asked the older girl about it and she led me downstairs to the full vintage Fisher Price "Little People Play Family Farm" with all of its pieces accounted for.

After the kids were deep in dreamland, I took the farm to their living room. I opened and closed the barn door over and over again, listening to the "moo" I had giggled at so many years before. This toy, which had once been a source of joy for me, was now a painful reminder of the past. And once again, I was broken. When Ann came home that night, she found me clenching the farm to my chest, lying in the fetal position on her living room floor.

Triggers like these are a frequent event. Any time I see a fire or hear the distinct roaring crackle I can instantly go into a panic or have an anxiety attack. It doesn't take much. I often have nightmares and still find myself crying at unpredictable moments.

I have come to accept that my life will never be the same. I will never return to the way things were before.

I will never be "normal" again. But I find hope in that. Even though this journey has been, by far, the longest and hardest experience I have ever had to face, I take encouragement that my awful circumstances are being used for a greater good. My new "normal" is greater than I could have ever imagined.

In three years, my family has built a brand new house which I have nicknamed "The Lodge." It is absolutely beautiful with a zip line and heated floors. I no longer have to worry about the foundation like I did in the past. We have a real furnace now! We have hot water! All luxuries that we never even dreamed of before the fire.

But I didn't just rebuild my home. I have rebuilt my life. I can't exactly pinpoint one specific experience in which I was able to hope again. It was a process. It was a long, hard journey that I am still walking. Once I realized that it was ok to be ok again, I was able to embrace the journey.

I still don't fully understand why things happened, but I realized that sometimes in waiting for answers, life only passes you by. I don't know why this happened to me. I don't know that I ever will. The pain is still with me, but the fog is lifting. I am able to remember the past while continuing to live in the present. I have the rest of my life in front of me, and I plan to live it to the fullest.

As I make the drive up the mountain, I am no longer plagued with memories of death and ashes all around me. The grass and trees have started to grow back. There is life shining through the darkness. Love is starting afresh with new possibilities, and life is beginning to rise from the ashes.

WALKING THROUGH FIRE

KRISTEN MOELLER

L eslie and I have carried and nurtured the dream of this book for well over a year. It was inventible that I write my story, yet after blogging extensively after the fire and then writing my second book with more tales from the fire, I was tired of telling the same story. Life was in transition, so I kept thinking if I waited *just a little longer* I would know what I needed to share.

At first, it was to be a tale of finally making the decision to rebuild after a year and a half of wandering and wondering if we would ever move forward. It would be the tale of our emotional—and hard-earned—return to the land, rising like the phoenix to emerge victorious. And all of this would be on national TV on a show called *Tiny House Nation*. But this "Cinderella story" turned out not to be the story I needed to tell at all.

When I lost my home to fire, I lost a part of myself as well. My home was our sanctuary. It was a place where we took refuge from the world, where I caught my breath with a deep sigh of relief each time I pulled in the driveway, a place where we healed from the dashed dreams of parenthood after losing a baby, a place where we grew together as a couple in ways that many people don't after walking through massive challenges in a marriage. It was a place where our friends gathered and felt their own internal angst recede, a place where they marveled at the beauty, as well as the mettle it took to live so far away from it all.

Down a mile-long private jeep trail of a road, completely off-grid and solar power only, it took grit to live there, a grit we found we had and we cultivated as the years went by. With only a woodstove for heat, we grumbled when we returned home on a frigid winter eve to a bitterly cold house and tossed wood on the stove as we ran upstairs to dive under a pile of comforters with only our noses exposed, waiting for the warmth to come. And we wouldn't have traded it for anything. When we first found it, we knew it was our forever home.

The raging wildfire that consumed our home also left twenty-one other families homeless, and three of our neighbors dead. A "controlled burn" gone bad, carelessly mismanaged by Colorado State Forest Service during a particularly dry March. It was an accident waiting to happen. And happen it did. Suddenly and unexpectedly the fire swept up our mountainside, carried by sixty mile-an-hour gusts; and while bureaucracies pointed fingers, the 911 systems broke down and fire department jurisdiction lines blurred, resulting in chaos instead of clarity of who was supposed to respond. A true, yet sadly preventable tragedy, it left a small community in tatters and devastation.

While dealing with the aftermath, David and I moved from friends' basements, to borrowed houses, to a vintage Airstream trailer on our burned-out land, back to basements. We battled against our insurance company and the state of Colorado, yet thankfully not each other.

We wept deeply and questioned everything. We were burned out on a profound level, exhausted to our core and wondered if we would ever truly be happy again.

At first, we were certain we would rebuild. Then after a long, hot summer of moving to and fro and coming in over budget with multiple builders one too many times, we gave up. We moved to a nearby town called Evergreen, to a house by a lake, tucked in a little neighborhood that held us well as we worked on healing our hearts.

We hoped that time would not only heal but that it would bring clarity, yet clarity seemed to allude us. *Should we return to the land? Should we sell? Should we build a cabin? What should we do?* Knowing that Evergreen was a temporary stop allowed us to fully enjoy it but never fully settle in.

In December of 2013, we found a company with adorable prefab cabins, and the wheels started turning in a new direction. After a sit down, some customization of plans and multiple heart-to-hearts, we decided to proceed down the cabin path. Then one day, our new cabin builders sent us an email that changed our direction again. The *Tiny House Nation* series was just launching and was seeking families who were trying out the tiny house lifestyle. Always adventurers, it seemed to be a sign from above—a poetic "full circle" story, where not only would we be returning to the land but we would be doing it on national TV.

We had been on camera quite a bit after the fire so it seemed like the perfect ending. Very rapidly, a decision was made: we would not only rebuild, we would try living "tiny"—and do it with cameras rolling. Everything accelerated as we headed toward a film date in June of 2014. Jumping into action, I focused all my energy on being the general contractor, learning as I went, gathering what I hoped was a solid team to take us through the build and our return home.

Finally the big day approached after many moments of wondering if we would make it and countless sleepless nights. With breakdowns galore in the form of crews working on top of each other, contractors who we trusted turning out to be unworthy of that trust, major construction issues, weather delays and more—it was tenuous at times and terrifying at others. But once the cameras started rolling, it all looked perfect and rosy— like the dream coming true.

It was exciting. It was a once in a lifetime experience. A beautiful story of our life and our life-altering event was told, yet after the filming ended and the TV crews packed up, the problems continued—and even seemed to multiply. Still we fully enjoyed living in our new space, back on the land in our "Tiny Mansion," as we called it, for at 700 square feet it was cheating to call it a true "tiny house." Returning to the land and living in a mini show home, we slowly unwound, spending sun drenched days on the patios and absorbing the deafening quiet, watching hawks circle, and smiling as the dogs finally had space to run and chase critters once again.

For a moment—or two—we caught our breath and lived a new life on our old land.

But the leaks continued, the appliances malfunctioned, the cracks in the concrete floor widened—and then the final straw—our Internet provider of eight years plus dropped us from their coverage area. Without working Internet or cell phones in our remote location, and as two entrepreneurs who work from home, this was a deal breaker. Exhausted, disheartened, baffled by the yellow brick road that led to nowhere, we screamed "uncle," packed up, and moved away.

As all this was happening, one of my soul-sister friends was receiving a diagnosis at age fifty of non-Hodgkin's lymphoma. Living three hours from her, we texted all the time, and she was hopeful of beating the odds. In great shape, psychologically strong with a tremendous support system, her docs told her that if anyone could beat it, it would be she.

On March 15, 2015, Denise took her last breaths, and I geared up for a time of mourning my beloved friend. Then, two days later on St Patrick's Day, my mother died unexpectedly. Six days after that, my twenty-eight-year-old champion motorcycle racer cousin died in a crash, after a lovely dinner out with his family.

During this new phase of upheaval, I started to believe that catching one's breath in life is only a fantasy.

Before the fire, life happened too, but in my old home I felt held by something I can't quite name. Without that container, I am in unfamiliar territory.

As I walked through my grief after the fire, I wrote my pain and hoped to make sense of the loss. The metaphors were obvious—the phoenix rising from the ashes as it sheds the old form and transforms into a new realm of existence. I wrote almost daily for a year, exploring the symbolism while letting myself be where I was no matter how messy it seemed. I let myself be undone, unraveled and raw—and I allowed the writing to ground me as I walked through the loss.

I now sit on my patio staring up at the tiny mansion that juts out a bluebird sky so typical of Colorado. To the left of the house stands our totem pole, a gift from David on our thirteen-year wedding anniversary. It remained standing after the fire, the front scorched black, the back hollowed out, its wings having fallen to the ground. At some point, it fell and rested in the dirt until, with cameras rolling, we resurrected it, reattached its wings, and gave it new life. It's even more beautiful than before.

It's eerie and scarred with faint remnants of white paint intermingled with charred ebony and raw wood patches. Sometimes I fear it will topple again as it sways while buffeted by the force of the ferocious winds that blow across our treeless land. If it falls again, I am not sure it will have another life.

The view from here is breathtaking, yet it's the totem pole that draws me in, especially today. It's Easter Sunday, a time of renewal and rebirth. Later we will celebrate with friends, but for now I sit in this place where we once lived and called home and now only visit. It's a place with many memories, where hopes and dreams were born, then crushed, then rediscovered. It's a place that my mother loved and visited years ago, and my dear friend Denise visited more recently. After the build, Denise joined me for a sleepover while David traveled. We lit the first bonfire in our new flagstone pit, erected like a sarcophagus atop our old simple stone campfire.

We watched the flames leap higher and higher, and I squirmed and allowed feelings of discomfort, deep sadness, and loss to arise and then float away on the embers. I imagined what it must have been like as my house was consumed after I fled—the dark cloud of smoke blotting out all light, the smoldering heat turning to a raging inferno that altered my life forever. Denise and I sat together, often silently as only old friends can, and stared at the flames into the night. We gazed at the stars partially obscured by smoke as we laughed and talked about this crazy little thing called life and all the twists and turns it takes.

Now I sit in the same place, six months later, with a heart-shaped urn filled with my mother's ashes. I hold it in my hand and pretend I am holding her hand. I crave the comfort and unconditional love of my mother. The new grief clutches at my chest and takes my breath away. So much has happened on this land and in my life. So much love, so much joy and so much sadness, loss, and tragedy.

This landscape is forever altered. Thousands of acres of once towering pines were reduced to blackened toothpicks, never to be green again. Yet in a month or so, the hillside will turn green. Fresh growth in the form of grass and wildflowers will transform the landscape and bring new life.

Today, we watch eagles soar high above and hawks wrestle airborne with ravens. We marvel at the view, stare off into the distance, and let the tears come. I am no more settled now than I was before. In fact, I am more unhinged and yet I am starting to think that may be OK. The sense of home I was seeking seems just out of reach, or perhaps something that will never be again. It is fleeting, faint, and slowly fading into the distance.

I will not spout platitudes about home being where my heart is, or where I lay my head. I will mourn the loss of home, the loss of my friend, the loss of my cousin, and I know I will forever mourn the loss of my mother.

I sought guarantees in life long after I knew life would not comply. Still reeling from these recent losses, I don't know where I will land in myself yet. What I do know is that when I turn to the page, and write my story, something makes sense, even if for only a moment.

As I read this story aloud to my husband, an eagle soars by our cliffside, mere feet below where we sit. He lands in a tree, his tree, his reclaimed home on this burned out land.

I return my gaze to the totem pole from my perch by my now bare fire pit. I think about the collection of women who have shared their stories in this book. I know that hearts are reached as our stories tell truths about what we hold precious, what we love, and what we fear. These stories provide snapshots into a variety of lives when time stood still, the world rocked on its orbit, and our hearts broke into pieces. I imagine us here together in a circle as a sisterhood of women, sharing our tales, sitting around the campfire, feeling the heat of life, and gaining comfort in being together. Maybe we don't need to catch our breath after all. Maybe sitting together and sharing our stories is enough.

ABOUT THE CONTRIBUTORS

Amanda DeAngelis is the owner of Nine Births Childbirth Services located in Fort Collins, Colorado. She works as a labor doula, childbirth educator, and midwife's assistant. For over five years she has dedicated herself to helping families bring their children into the world peacefully. She spends most of her days walking in the woods, painting, and loving on her incredible children, husband, and dogs. Amanda and her husband were building their house when the High Park fire broke out in 2012. Their home was spared.

Ann Lansing is the owner of Lansing Design, an Interior Design Firm based in Boulder Colorado. She loves to travel and works on designs for homes all over the world. Her new home is nestled in the foothills of the mountains she loves in Boulder, Colorado. Ann lost her home of many years to the Four Mile Canyon fire in 2010.

AnnMarie Arbo is a caseworker for the Long Term Recovery Team in Larimer County, Colorado. Ann Marie immigrated to the United States from Great Britain thirty years ago and has since worked in the helping profession with homeless people and disaster survivors. As she helped families who lost homes in the fires of 2012, the floods of 2013 added even more new families to her caseload. Her story depicts both the heartbreak and inner strength that is forged by fire.

Astrid is a successful businesswoman, owning and managing all-inclusive properties for low-income singles and families in Colorado. Not only did her cabin in the foothills burn in the High Park fire of 2012, but also flooding the following year displaced five of her tenants. Astrid is a shining star who shows strength and resilience in recovering loss both for herself and others.

Barbara Nickless promised her mother she'd be a novelist when she grew up—because what could be safer than sitting at a desk all day? But an English degree and graduate work in physics took her down other paths—technical writer, raptor rehabilitator, astronomy instructor, sword fighter, piano teacher, and journalist. Now an award-winning writer, she spends her free time caving, snowshoeing, and hiking the Colorado fourteeners. She and her husband live in Colorado Springs, Colorado, where in June of 2012 they lost their home of twenty-two years to the Waldo Canyon fire.

Bethany Trantham is an eighteen-year-old senior at Regis Jesuit High School. She enjoys history and English—and is a blossoming writer as well. To walk through her experience with fire, she relied on her Christian faith. She was especially helped by a devotional which her pastor gave her entitled, "When Your Whole World Changes," and the verse Psalm 46:10, "Be still, and know that I am God." For fun, she loves zip lining at her family cabin in the mountains and creating music. Her mother, Yvette Trantham, is also a contributing author in this book.

As an educator in the public school system for over forty years, **Beth Cutter** worked with colleagues and students from the Black Forest, an area north of Colorado Springs. She and her husband Steve raised their family there. At the tail end of a fun-filled weekend in 2013 spent with their grandchildren, the Black Forest fire broke out. They evacuated with their three dogs and their laptops. Only memories remained of their home after it burned to the ground. They have since rebuilt on the same site. Although "retired," Beth teaches for the College of Education at the University of Colorado in Colorado Springs.

Bonnie Antich owns an art gallery in downtown Fort Collins by the same name as her story, the Canyon Spirit Gallery. A firefighter for four years in her early thirties, she is now a potter and her husband Scotty makes one-of-a-kind furniture. Both delight in the use of natural materials in their art, such as moose hair in the firing of the pottery and twigs and branches in the furniture. Bonnie is also a telemark skier, gardener, hiker, and stargazer—and she is learning to play the ukulele.

Born in San Antonio, Texas, **Cheryl Delany** began her artistic career around the age of eight. She drew illustrations for a book written by her one-year older sister. Now all grown up, she enjoys writing uplifting stories filled with comedy, romance, fun, and adventure. Her latest romantic comedy entitled *Bully U* can be found on Amazon. Cheryl lives with her husband Isaac in the foothills southwest of Denver.

Jackie Klausmeyer teaches math and science to at-risk youth. She enjoys gardening, horses, birdwatching, RAIN! And doing just about anything outdoors in her free time. For more than thirty years, Jackie has lived in and loved the foothills. Then in 2012, she and her husband Randy Pierce lost their home, barn, shop, and all their belongings to the High Park Fire. Rebuilding the house themselves, they hope to move into their beautiful new home in the summer of 2015.

Jenn Nolte, RN, BSN, works with at risk patients as part of a physician residency program in Fort Collins, Colorado. Always having loved the wilderness and being surrounded by nature, she and her husband re-energize by backpacking, canoeing, and going on road trips. The High Park fire of 2012 claimed their newly built home, homemade timber frame shed, and beloved land. They were one week away from their certificate of occupancy. Since the fire, they have rebuilt and have been enjoying their new home since 2014.

Kendra Eucker wrote about her harrowing experience in the Lower North Fork fire of 2012. She didn't lose her home but she came close to losing everything else. A recent college graduate with a Bachelor of Science in biology, she has a passion for wildlife, science, and the outdoors. She is planning on going back to school to get her master's degree in wildlife biology. Kendra was recently engaged and is currently working on plans for her upcoming wedding.

Linda Masterson is the author of *Surviving Wildfire. Get Prepared. Stay Alive. Rebuild Your Life*, a handbook for homeowners living with the risk of wildfire, and the *Living with Bears* handbook, a practical guide for coexisting with bears. Linda is a popular speaker and was most recently a featured presenter at the national Firewise Backyards and Beyond Conference. She left a communications career in Chicago to follow her heart to a new life in the mountains she loved. She's a partner in Masterson & Phillips, a communications firm. Linda lost her home in the Crystal Mountain fire in 2011.

Louise Creager works as a real estate broker in Fort Collins, Colorado. Louise specializes in helping people buy mountain property. Her volunteer efforts help support the local volunteer fire department. Her husband built their home in Rist Canyon, which was consumed by the High Park fire in 2012. They are rebuilding a new home on the same land.

Born in Texas but raised in Louisiana, **Melissa Fry** spent years living in New Orleans working in the music and event industries before moving to Colorado after Hurricane Katrina. After seven years in the advertising industry, she recently semi-retired and now teaches Ashtanga yoga in Boulder, Colorado. Melissa and her husband Evan Fry lost their home in the Four Mile Canyon fire in 2010. She now lives outside of Boulder up Sunshine Canyon with her husband and their two mutts, Donnie and George.

Susan Ruane McConnell is the owner of Soul Style Home, a business that provides a unique process for people to re-imagine and reinvent home as an authentic, beautiful and soul-nurturing space. She is a freelance marketing resource for business, civic, and nonprofit groups. She served as managing editor and feature writer for two city magazines, and was principal writer for several business books as well as *Public Treasures: Outdoor Sculpture in the Pikes Peak Region*. Susan lost her home in the Waldo Canyon fire in 2012. By applying her professional expertise to her personal life, she now lives again in a soul-nurturing home in Colorado Springs.

Firefighter **Sandi Yukman** has literally walked through fire. Sandi fought fires as a member of the Colorado Springs Utilities Catamount Wildland Fire team for eight years, most notably the devastating Waldo Canyon fire. Now retired, the Colorado mountains are her playground.

She loves hiking, snowboarding, and ice climbing and has climbed all of the fifty-nine Colorado fourteeners. When she's not traveling with her husband, her home base is Colorado Springs.

Yvette Trantham is a Colorado native. Her family purchased a cabin in the mountains in 1975. It was destroyed in the Lower North Fork Fire in 2012. She is a graduate of Columbine High School and is an engineering graduate from the University of Colorado, Boulder. She works as an engineer in the aerospace industry. Yvette lives in Aurora with her husband and three children. She spends as much free time as possible in the mountains. Her dream is to someday retire and live full time in the family home on the mountain.

About the Authors

Leslie Aplin Wharton and her husband Mark lost their home in the High Park fire in 2012. Concerned with how their lives impacted the planet, they built their house to be off-grid solar and heated by the sun. Leslie helped her husband, a general contractor and potter, build homes and design and install solar electric systems.

Leslie's love for the outdoors has always guided her career choices, which in Colorado included running camps and selling outdoor gear. She was the manager of the camping department at Jax Outdoor Gear in Fort Collins, Colorado, when the fire happened. After the fire, Leslie and Mark moved to Bellingham, Washington, and reinvented themselves.

Along with writing a memoir and coauthoring and gathering stories and poems for *Phoenix Rising*, she is now a caregiver for the elderly. She loves to hear the important stories of their lives and has learned that if you live to ninety, it's likely you've lived through a tragedy.

In Colorado, Leslie was an avid telemark skier, rock and ice climber, whitewater paddler, and backpacker. In Washington, she prefers less adrenaline and spends her free time fishing, gardening, hiking, and listening to the frogs.

You can learn more about Leslie by visiting her website at www. EdgeofNext.com.

After losing her dream home and all her worldly possessions to the Lower North Fork fire that killed three people and demolished twenty-one homes, **Kristen Moeller** was at a crossroads. Drawing on twenty-five years of training in psychology and personal growth, as well as her own recovery from addiction in 1989, Kristen dove headfirst into an exploration of our cultural discomfort with grief, finding humor in the midst of tragedy—and what it means to be a human being with all our fabulousness as well as frailties.

A bestselling author, book publisher, TEDx speaker, and radio show host with a master's degree in counseling, Kristen has a passion for championing those who become lost in their wild journey through this wacky world. After a fresh round of devastating losses, she now specializes in working with women over fifty who are writing a Legacy books.

After appearing on A&E's *Tiny House Nation*, Kristen realized that returning "full circle" in life is mostly a fantasy. She now runs writing retreats at her "Tiny Mansion" and lives in Salida, Colorado, with her husband of twenty years, their two big dogs, and an ornery cat named Bill. Her most recent book is *What Are You Waiting For? How to Rise to the Occasion of Your Life* (Viva Editions).

You can find out more about Kristen by visiting her website at www. KristenMoeller.com.

PHOTO ALBUM

New meets Old—Kristen

Kristen's house before

Kristen's house after

Remnants of Kristen's dream house

Foundation after cleanout—Kristen

*Dream house
in danger—
Jenn Nolte*

*Utter destruction and heartbreak,
Nolte home after the fire*

High Park fire Memorial sign at entrance of Rist Canyon, CO
—Jenn Nolte

After the fire, comes new hazards
—Jenn Nolte

Burnt book of Leslie's

*A Favorite Tree
of Leslie's*

Cutter grandchildren's first visit to home site

Cutter site after demolition

Leslie on the first day back at the house site. Holding on to hope

Leslie's kitchen

Leslie's husband Mark's
pottery. Glazes melt at
2200 degrees so the fire
was at least that hot

Letting Go—Amanda DeAngelis

Walking on the Moon—Amanda DeAngelis

Sandi Yukman working a Prescribed Burn

Susan McConnell surveys the devastation

Susan McConnell's destroyed property

Surprise survivor—Susan McConnell

This way to disaster—Susan McConnell

Starting from scratch - Susan McConnell

Louise Creager's new home

Melissa Fry on the deck of her new home

Trantham cabin before fire

*Trantham cabin
after fire*

*Above: Linda Masterson
and her husband Cory
after the fire
Right: Green shoot
through rock and ash—
Astrid*

The Barge—Jackie Klausmeyer

PHOENIX RISING FUND

Twenty percent of author proceeds will be donated to the Phoenix Rising Fund, which provides scholarships to therapeutic writing programs for women who are dealing with natural disasters. For more information, please visit www.PhoenixRisingFund.com